Also by Mark Haskell Smith

Fiction

Moist
Delicious
Salty
Baked
Raw: A Love Story
Blown

Nonfiction

Heart of Dankness
Naked at Lunch

RUDE TALK IN ATHENS

Ancient Rivals, the Birth of Comedy, and a Writer's Journey through Greece

MARK HASKELL SMITH

The Unnamed Press
Los Angeles, CA

You will never create anything great by drinking water.
—Attributed to Cratinus, fifth century BCE

RUDE TALK IN ATHENS

An Introductory Scene

The Meltemi was not fucking around. We had intended to sail in the morning, from Koufonisia to Iraklia, but the fierce seasonal wind that torments these islands, the Aegean version of the Santa Ana winds in Los Angeles, had other ideas. A small craft warning had been issued. We were stuck. Not that anyone complained. Why set out in heavy seas for a beautiful Greek island when you're already on a beautiful Greek island?

Better to live in the moment, which is easy to do when there's a bar that, every day at sunset, lays cushions along a stone jetty so that you can have a drink and watch the daylight fade. As the sun drops behind the horizon, the light cuts through a channel between two islands, plunging the undulating hills into a deep purple while the sea shimmers and the sky glows violet and rosé. Or maybe that was the wine. It really wasn't an inconvenience. When life gives you a glass of rosé, order a bottle.

Koufonisia is a small island in a string of small islands in what is called the Lesser Cyclades in the Aegean Sea. It's a few hours by ferry from Athens, not far from Naxos, which is larger and part of the regular Cyclades. The small island that turned purple, only a few hundred meters away, was inhabited solely by goats.

The air was fresh, the wine was cold and delicious, and the smell of grilling fish was drifting from the kitchen of a nearby taverna. I was with my wife and some friends, and we were relaxed and happy. If it sounds idyllic, it was. In that moment, life felt extremely pleasurable. I thought, Why isn't *this* the goal of human existence? Not necessarily this island or this rosé or these friends, but the feeling of pleasure, the joy at being alive in the world. Why can't we arrange society so that everyone can experience this feeling most of the time? We could, you know, if we weren't so busy chasing a dollar, extracting the life out of the planet, and dropping bombs on each other. And for what? Why the unrelenting hustle? You can't put a sunset or friendship or a summer breeze on your credit card. Which is not to say that the journey to this spot was free, but there are sunsets and friends and breezes in Los Angeles that are right outside my door. Why do we devote our lives to activities and objects that don't bring us pleasure?

I am not the first person to have this thought. Around 311 BCE, a Greek philosopher named Epicurus believed that pleasure should be the highest goal of humanity. He described the three main ingredients for happiness as friendship, disengagement from material concerns, and free time to pursue your own interests. In other words, live communally with people you like, free your mind from the delusion that objects or money or fame will make you happy, and take time for contemplation, for walks in nature, for reading and art. This simple philosophy became extremely popular in ancient Greece, and by the first century CE there were approximately a half million people living in Epicurean communes throughout the Mediterranean. A couple thousand years after Epicurus laid out his ideas, an economist in London named Karl Marx used it as inspiration for a very similar societal model he called "communism."

Epicurus was not a food snob or wine aficionado. By his own accounts he lived simply, preferring lentils and bread to lavish banquets. How he became associated with luxury goods, brand ambassadors, ortolan gobblers, and, for want of a better word, assholes is a consequence of the Catholic Church's two-thousand-year smear campaign against him and his followers. That's because Epicurus had no time for deities, he was all about simple pleasure and contemplation in the here and now. He didn't believe in the afterlife. As he wrote, "When we exist,

Parodos

Ancient Greek comedies start with a prologue, a brief introductory scene that sets up the story and provides a little context for what follows. The previous chapter was the prologue. What happens next is the parodos, the entry of the chorus, a moment when the costumes are revealed. Sometimes there's a little song or a dance that sets the vibe for the performance. A chorus is fundamental to early Greek comedies; it is essentially a troupe that takes to the stage at various times to perform musical numbers and interact with the actors. Often it breaks the fourth wall and speaks directly to the audience.

I have no song or dance. I'm not wearing a colorful costume. And this kind of writing is all about breaking the fourth wall. This parodos takes the form of a disclaimer disguised as an anecdote.

I used to visit a mechanic in Frogtown, a neighborhood in northeast Los Angeles by the L.A. River notable for warehouses, light industry, and the old Holland Dutch Bakery. He was a self-styled anarchist, an excellent mechanic, and an all-around kind and generous eccentric named Pete. Perhaps because he was a Volkswagen mechanic of a certain generation, he chafed at things like business licenses and bookkeeping practices. He wanted to do his own thing without any oversight from the government, and so on his receipts it said:

Incompetent Free Man — Trying To Help
My Word Your Only Guarantee — Payment Not Required

He didn't charge money for his services but accepted "non-deductible donations of Federal Reserve notes." If you were between paychecks or waiting for your next Hollywood deal to come through, he'd fix your car and you could pay him when you could. No interest, no deposit, no questions. He also had a bumper sticker on his car that said: GOD SAVE ME FROM YOUR FOLLOWERS. Which may, later, have some relevance to this story. Although you have presumably paid money for this book, I'm going to offer a similar disclaimer, not that I can trouble-shoot your clutch or change your spark plugs, but that I am an incompetent-free human, not a scholar of ancient Greece. I don't read classical or modern Greek and I never undertook any serious study of the classics when I was in college. I'm not even sure the classics were offered at my college. The sections of this book that are historical re-creations are based on information that I have pulled from various sources, trying to paint a picture of Athenian life circa 420 BCE, and just like a cheesy re-creation on the History Channel, some artistic license has been taken.

Scholars of ancient Greece might be put off by what I'm attempting here and I'm okay with that. This is not a book of scholarship. It is more of a ramble through a time and a place than an academic work. It is a speculative biography. Kind of. And while a professor with a Ph.D. in classical studies may be able to read the texts in ancient Greek, while she may be able to parse the historical context of the humor, classicists aren't comedy writers. I've written several novels—and a couple of movies and plays—that aspire to be comedies. I know what it's like to earn a living writing comedy. It's a weird job, trying to squeeze a laugh out of a fellow human being, and it comes with as many perils and pleasures as you'd expect. So while I may not have memorized passages of Homer, for better or worse, the skill set that I'm bringing to this project is my curiosity and the ability to be occasionally entertaining.

If you're unfamiliar with the world of ancient Athens, then you're in for a treat, because it is a fascinating and rich period of human history. A time and a place where representative democracy, free speech, and comedy all took root. I wouldn't be writing this book—or any book like the kinds of books I write—without Athenians standing up and demanding to control their own destiny. Joined in a common cause, they fought against monarchs and oligarchs and tribal traditions, they came together and proclaimed a revolutionary idea: the essential right to have a voice in the decisions that governed their lives and to express themselves freely and without fear. Heroically, once they had secured these hard-earned freedoms, they began making jokes about farts and boners.

At the Symposium

"Acropolis" is a Greek word that breaks down as *akro*, "highest" or "topmost," and *polis*, "city." It's typically a hill with sheer cliffs and steep slopes, enabling residents to drop heavy objects and rain fire on any invaders who might be coming to sack the town and enslave them. It was a useful advantage back in the day, and there are a surprising number of acropoleis scattered around Greece. But just like when New Yorkers say "the city," they mean Manhattan and not Queens, when people say "the Acropolis" they are referring to the Acropolis of Athens. That's because it's crowned by the Parthenon, the ancient temple of the goddess Athena. You might not be able to find Greece on a map, but you will have seen an image of the Parthenon.

The Parthenon (*Wikimedia Commons*).

T-shirts, key chains, bottle openers, those paper cups you get from Greek diners, and all kinds of replica statues made out of injection-molded plastics can be found with the image of the Parthenon. It is one of the most iconic icons in the world. It is also the defining symbol of the city of Athens. The municipality doesn't allow buildings over a certain height because it wants everyone to have a view of it. Walk around Athens after dark and it's impossible to miss the Parthenon glowing on top of the Acropolis. Maybe it's just me, someone who lives in Los Angeles, where they could turn the Hollywood sign into a singing and dancing laser light spectacular and I wouldn't look up, but seeing the Parthenon at night makes me stop in my tracks. More than beautiful; somehow resonant and mysterious.

At the base of the Acropolis, close to the ruins of the ancient Theater of Dionysus, is the Acropolis Museum, which opened in 2009. Compared with the jumbled-up buildings of the surrounding area, the museum is a sleek and beautiful repository for the sculptures, archaeological objects, and marble friezes left behind after a British earl named Thomas Bruce looted the Parthenon in the early 1800s.* When construction of the museum began—in a discovery that didn't surprise a single archaeologist—builders found the ruins of a neighborhood thousands of years old on the site.

As you can imagine, this kind of find is not uncommon in Athens. When it's not looming over the city from the Acropolis, the ancient world is underfoot everywhere. During construction of the subway system, excavation crews uncovered ancient rivers, villas, workshops, brothels, taverns—all kinds of remnants of a robust civilization. Many of these structures they left in situ in the stations, turning the underground into public archaeological museums. The past has even been assimilated into retail environments: for example there's a Zara store with a glass floor where you can look down into a Roman mausoleum built on top of a Greek mausoleum, which is probably on top of some other

---

* The looted artifacts from this smash and grab were renamed the Elgin Marbles and are on display at the British Museum, as if they were property of the British, who should really give them back.

structure, which is, as some Americans might tell you, built on the field where Jesus used to ride a *Triceratops* for fun.

The past is inescapable, and that is part of the city's charm. Athenians manage to live alongside the ancient world without any problem. When the Acropolis Museum architects discovered the ruins of a thriving neighborhood on their site, they didn't freak out; they turned it into an exhibit. Now you can walk underneath the museum and see the remnants of old sewers and drains, modest houses and slightly larger villas. Including a home with an *andron*.

An *andron* was a room used exclusively by men for manly things, like getting wasted and talking about sports and politics. It was the original man cave—although now that I say that, there were probably men-only caves back in Paleolithic times where men got wasted on fermented fruit and swapped Paleo diet tips. But back in the fifth century BCE, almost every successful Athenian had some version of an *andron* in his home. The *andron* under the Acropolis Museum has remnants of mosaic floor and the benches set into the walls that were required for a proper symposium.

A symposium is not, as I had always thought, a tedious academic conference where papers on obscure topics are delivered in droning monotone, but a drinking party. The etymology in ancient Greek looks like this: *sum-* (together) + *potēs* (drinker) = *sumpotēs*, or "fellow drinker." Later it became "symposium." It turns out I have been attending symposia my entire adult life. I am quite good at symposiuming.

Men would gather in the *andron*, wine mixed with water would be served, maybe some snacks, and they would talk. These drinking parties, like all drinking parties, started out with small talk—maybe about poetry and love or the price of anchovies—and then, like all drinking parties, either fizzled out completely or turned into a rager. My favorite line from Plato's *Symposium*, an account of a drinking party celebrating the victory of the poet Agathon at the Lenaia festival in 416 BCE, is not the speech by Socrates or Aristophanes's lovely depiction of the origins of sexual attraction, but from Alcibiades,* who arrives late, already half in the bag, and announces with great gusto, "Good evening, gentlemen. I'm plastered."[1]

The *andron* under the Acropolis Museum (*photograph by Diana Faust*).

The *andron* was reserved for male bonding, but that doesn't mean that there weren't women present. Any decent symposium would feature singing, dancing, drink-pouring sex workers called "flute girls."

Flute girls were likely slaves owned by one of the local brothels, which is not to say that they weren't musicians or to imply that they were all prostitutes. In fact, there is some debate

---

*A wealthy and extremely good-looking Athenian born in 450 BCE, Alcibiades was kind of a rock star until he led an expedition to Sicily in 415 BCE, where the Greek army got its ass handed to it.

about this among historians. We do know that they were trained to play an aulos, which was a double-reeded, double-bodied flute—kind of like having two oboes jammed into your mouth at the same time. Playing this tricky instrument was a skill that I imagine took considerable practice to master. Many scholars relegate flute girls to the role of sex workers who played some tunes and then provided a happy finish to the evening's entertainment. And this may have been true. But history has been written by men, and men don't really give women credit for their accomplishments. And, like a lot of things about Athenian society at that time, we don't really know, so let's just say that in a kind of crazy twist, flute girls were both musicians and groupies, and it was not unusual for them to be enslaved.

Let's imagine our subject, Ariphrades, arriving for a symposium in the Plaka neighborhood of Athens, not far from the Acropolis and the Agora, the central marketplace, circa 420 BCE. Let's say the symposium is hosted by a wealthy patron of the arts and, much like a literary salon in Paris or a coffee shop in Brooklyn, the room is filled with writers and their egos—with a few flute girls squeezed in for imaginary historical accuracy.

Ariphrades stood outside the house and adjusted his chiton. He wasn't cold, but in this well-to-do part of the Plaka he wanted to look sharp, so he threw part of the cloth over his shoulder, pulling it down and tucking it into a fold. He ran his fingers through his beard and smoothed his hair. He really should've cleaned up and changed into fresh clothes before coming to such an auspicious gathering, but he'd been preoccupied, working on a new play, before joining his brothers at the palaestra for some exercise. He sniffed his armpits. They smelled like fresh olive oil.

An enslaved young man answered the door and Ariphrades couldn't help but feel underdressed. Even the slave's clothing was of finer quality than his. He wiped his bare feet and followed him through the house to where the symposium was under way.

Oil lamps lit the crowded *andron*, and Ariphrades could see several famous writers reclining on the couches as the wine flowed.

Let's imagine that the host of this symposium loved the theater and bankrolled the productions at the festivals. Who else might have been in the room? Perhaps a young man named Eupolis, who had won first prize at the previous year's City Dionysia with his comedy *Toadies*. Maybe Leucon, who came in third that year. Other comedy writers, like Pherecrates and Philonides, would probably be here. Agathon the poet. Perhaps the famous tragedians Sophocles and Euripides were lounging in a corner. Just because their plays are heavy doesn't mean they don't like to party.

Unless you're a classicist or a scholar of ancient Athenian comedy, these names probably don't mean much to you. For most of them, today their work exists only in fragments or not at all. Which is not to say they weren't as important or successful or brilliant as Aristophanes at the time; it's just that for reasons we can speculate on later, history has been cruel.

Eupolis's *Toadies*, for example, sounds like something Phoebe Waller-Bridge or Molière might have written. A "toady" was a parasite, a moocher of the highest order. The play is about the wealthiest man in Athens inviting a bunch of intellectuals and their loser friends to his estate. High jinks, and the complete looting of his wealth, ensue. Here's a fragment that survived:

> *Now we'll tell you about the toady's life.*
> *Just listen how totally cool we really are:*
> *First of all, check out the servant we have with us;*
> *Usually it's someone else's boy, though I get my turn too.*
> *And I've got these two fancy coats, see*

I wear one of the other when I go to the marketplace.
And when I see some sucker there,
especially a rich one, I'm all over him!
And if this rich bozo utters so much as a syllable, I applaud it,
and pretend to be amazed at his every word.[2]

I can't imagine that every guest at this symposium was a writer. Hopefully our host would know better. An actor or musician or artist or philosopher might have been invited. Maybe a soldier or gentleman farmer. Definitely Aristophanes would be there, still smoldering with rage for coming in second to Eupolis at the last competition.

To give you some perspective of how important theater and writers were to ancient Athenians, what level celebrities they were at the time, this would've been akin to going to a party with Beyoncé and Bono, Guillermo del Toro and Paolo Sorrentino, Léa Seydoux and Elisabeth Moss, Taylor Swift, Tom Hanks, and the guy who sang "Gangnam Style," with maybe Padma Lakshmi, Damien Hirst, David Guetta, Formula One champion Lewis Hamilton, and the singer from Destroyer tossed into the mix for fun. In other words, they were the entertainment industry of their time, influential and important in the cultural and civic life of their community. Aside from sporting events and war, theater was what brought Athenians together, and comedy was the main outlet for unfiltered political speech that could reach a large audience. Have writers ever had it so good?

Platonius, a literary critic who historians believe was writing in the ninth or tenth century, wrote an essay called "On the Distinctions among Comedies," which described this particular era of Athenian comedy—so-called Old Comedy—as being uniquely rude: "And so, since free speech was available to all, writers of comedies had licence to mock generals and jurors who were making bad judgments and some of the citizens who were money-grubbers or lived licentiously."[3] Platonius reviewed the major works of the writers of this era and described Cratinus as particularly caustic, while Aristophanes softened his abuse with tongue-in-cheek humor. Eupolis, he says, was "as charming as he is sublime."[4]

Cratinus, widely known as a lover of wine with a taste for pretty boys, was older than both Eupolis and Aristophanes and had passed away by the time our imaginary symposium is happening. But if he had been alive, I'm confident he wouldn't have missed an opportunity to drink.

Like most artistic communities, I assume everyone knew everyone. Ariphrades would've smiled as he entered, and the other guests would've lifted their cups in greeting.

Ariphrades was handed a cup of wine and took a sip. The wine was from Chios—expensive and mixed with fresh spring water; it went down easily. Perhaps that accounted for the state of drunkenness in the *andron*.

Aristophanes was teetering in the center of the room, his beard soggy and stained from the grape, as an enslaved man refilled his cup. He began complaining about the size of tripods—the large trophies for theatrical competitions—being erected on the Street of Tripods. His last sponsor had declined to pay for one as large as Aristophanes felt he deserved. "Was that not the greatest comedy ever performed?" he asked the room.

One of the other writers present, maybe Leucon, said, "But you didn't win. So shut up."

Aristophanes ignored him and slurred, "Talent such as mine deserves the biggest tripod!"

Ariphrades saw some smirks from the other men, and a few shook their heads in dismay at Aristophanes's bragging. Most of them had heard it before; when Aristophanes was in his cups he could be a bit of a blowhard. But no one said anything, not even in jest, because Aristophanes was a cruel wit, the master of the sick burn, and no one wanted to be the target of one of his harangues.

Earlier in the evening there might have been talk of poetry and art, or the latest gossip about certain philosophers speaking at the stoa, but now, as the wine worked its magic and the flute girls circulated, the symposium was turning ever so slightly Dionysian.

Ariphrades watched the enslaved man scoop wine from the krater. And, as he waited for his cup to be refilled, he greeted the host and apologized for being late. The host patted the seat next to him, offering to share his couch. Ariphrades happily joined him, but as he sat he saw Aristophanes catch his eye across the room.

Aristophanes looked at the host and warned, "You might share your couch, but do not share your wine cup." Aristophanes laughed at his own comment, managing to spill some wine on his chiton in the process. He stepped into the center of the *andron* and raised his cup in a mocking toast. "Ariphrades the wicked. Greetings."

Ariphrades smiled and raised his cup to Aristophanes.

Aristophanes acknowledged him with a nod and asked, "And why were you late Ariphrades? Did something come up?" Aristophanes made a crude grab at his crotch, miming an uncontrollable erection and evoking peals of laughter from the guests.

Symposiuming (*Wikimedia Commons*).

Obviously I have no way of knowing if Aristophanes made these jokes at a symposium, but it's not much of a stretch because these are things Aristophanes said about Ariphrades in his plays; he was obsessed with Ariphrades, an exceptional personal and artistic vendetta that spanned more than thirty years of creative output. But tonight, at the imaginary symposium, he was just warming up. Another voice would jump in. Perhaps someone would agree with Aristophanes or Ariphrades might defend himself. Voices would be raised. People would mock and laugh and take the piss. In other words, a serious slanging match would erupt. Because that's what these guys did. Their plays were raunchy—explicitly sexual and scatological—and contained elements of what we call "battle rap"; it is easy to imagine insults, boasts, sexual innuendo, and imaginary scenarios involving your mother spilling from their mouths as the symposium got heated. That's because the comic playwrights of ancient Athens did not have a fuck to give about who they offended. It was the age of rude talk.

Athens™®

Classical Athens was built on the backs of slaves. The society was funded by conquest and constant war and ruled by a deeply entrenched patriarchy. It wasn't all poets and philosophers in sandals thinking groovy thoughts while naked young men wrestled in the palaestrae. Although that was part of it too. But in reality, as classics professor Johanna Hanink writes in her book *The Classical Debt*, Athens was "a well-oiled imperial machine."[1]

I'm not going to be an apologist for a slave-based economy or quote some historians who claim Athenians treated their slaves better than other civilizations did theirs. They enslaved the people they conquered. Period. Their standard of living was based on owning other human beings who did much of the hard labor, domestic duties, and basically all the shit work that the citizens didn't want to do. Almost every family had slaves, and some estimates put the ratio of slave to citizen at almost twenty to one. Those amazing buildings and monuments that tourists travel around the world to visit, the structures that we hold up as evidence of the superiority of Western civilization, much like the White House in Washington, D.C.—those were built by enslaved people. Which is not to diminish their grandeur or importance, but they were built to project the power of Athens to the ancient world. It worked at the time and continues to this day. Classical Athens is generally regarded as the birthplace of democracy, philosophy, theater, and the arts. Hanink continues in her book: "Athenians did not consciously 'invent' Western civilization, but they did consciously create an idealized vision of themselves and their city." In other words, they created a brand.

I wish I could buy into the myth of the utopian society where everyone wore organic linen and drank biodynamic wine while they discussed the life of the mind and read poetry, but fifth-century BCE Athens was complicated—sophisticated and beautiful and ugly and barbaric.

With the enslaved population taking care of the day-to-day chores, the male citizens of Athens devoted their energies to philosophy, the arts, politics, and the pursuit of pleasure. One of the things they did, in addition to getting plastered at tavernas and symposiums, was to enjoy a robust sex life. To paraphrase Demosthenes, you could have sex with a courtesan for pleasure, your wife to create heirs, and slaves for your daily sexual needs.[2]

Wives were for bearing offspring and managing the house, which gave them some agency—a distinctly different experience compared with the life of your average prostitute. We know that wives were protected and often confined to their homes so that the parentage of the offspring would not be questioned. Adultery was illegal, punishable by death. If you caught your wife having an affair, the Athenian courts allowed you to shove a radish up the offending man's ass. I'm not talking about one of those little French Breakfast radishes either; think daikon.

Prostitution was much like our modern customer rewards programs, with silver, gold, and platinum levels: a tiered system from expensive courtesans called "hetaerae," to flute girls who would entertain at parties, to brothel prostitutes, to streetwalkers who worked in the alleys and open areas of the Kerameikos. Socrates is famously quoted as saying the abundance of prostitutes was convenient as a kind of safety valve for releasing the pressures of lust.[3]

None of this was illegal or particularly frowned upon. Prices for various sex acts were set by the city government, which, naturally, was a group of men. And if that didn't float your boat, there were boys available for courting. Or you could just rub one out in public, as Diogenes the Cynic often did. When his fellow Athenians complained about his public masturbation, he famously wished, "it were as easy to banish hunger by rubbing the belly."[4] In other words, for men, it was an all-day splooge-a-thon; for women, who had virtually no rights in Athenian society, well, they were simply fucked. It was patriarchy on steroids. And all this sex on the brain had an impact on the arts.

Both of the major theater festivals, the Dionysia and the Lenaia, were centerpieces of a celebration of Dionysus, the god of wine and winemaking, fertility and epiphany, ecstasy and theater. And how better to start a celebration of this louche and irresistible god but with a phallus procession: a penis parade of drunk men carrying large cocks and shouting obscenities as they cavorted through town like some kind of raucous frat party or a convention of drunk regional marketing managers set loose in Vegas.

Some historians, including Aristotle, suggested that comedy was born from these debauched happenings. Which makes sense. They'd already gone to the trouble of making gigantic phalli for the parades, so why not put them to use in a more structured way? And it's the Dionysus festival. A party! After all, Dionysus was called "the god who comes." Some historians attribute this to some sort of epiphanic quality he possessed, but who are they kidding? He may inspire an epiphany, but then he rolls over and goes to sleep.

Still, the festivals were more than just drunken sausage parties; they were an opportunity for Athens to project its power and importance and show off its freewheeling culture to visitors from other parts of the world, especially ambassadors from conquered territories who were required to drop by and pay their annual taxes. Kind of like a Mob boss taking his tribute, then inviting you to stay for coffee and tiramisu.

The biggest event in Athens was the Panathenaic festival, which was held in the summer and was all about Athena. There were a lot of sacrifices of animals, which sounds messy. And I imagine it was slightly more respectful and restrained than the Dionysian festivals. The main feature of the festival was the procession from the Dipylon gate at the edge of the city, along the Panathenaic Way, to the top of the Acropolis. This parade is depicted in the frieze on the inner chamber of the Parthenon, somewhat disappointingly bereft of giant phalli. But this was still ancient Athens and they loved games and competitions, so the Panathenaic featured lots of sporting events like wrestling and boxing and chariot races. There were singing contests and epic poetry recitations. It sounds kind of like a county fair to me: a parade, some livestock, and funnel cakes.

But for theater-loving Athenians, the City Dionysia (held in the spring) and the Lenaia festival (sometime in mid-winter) were the highlights of the year. I should note that just like Broadway shows doing out-of-town tryouts, there was a festival held outside Athens sometime in December / January-ish, called the Rural Dionysia, where plays could be worked on far from the critical eye of sophisticated urbanites. The City Dionysia ran for five days with roughly three days for tragedies and two for comedy, while the Lenaia was a smaller festival that featured more comedies.

Who went to these plays? Well, according to David Kawalko Roselli, author of the book *Theater of the People: Spectators and Society in Ancient Athens*, almost everyone. In his book, Roselli endeavors to understand the politics of ancient Athens by figuring out who was attending the plays and how the content of the plays might've affected the populace. He believes the audiences were more mixed and international than previous historians have thought. "The diverse ethnic origins of the 'theater workers' (e.g., musicians), various financial sponsors, and trainers, as well as the participation of slaves, put a significant noncitizen presence right at the heart of theater production."[5]

If the population of Athens at the time was roughly three hundred thousand, and only thirty thousand were citizens, restricting the theatrical audience to male citizens doesn't make box office sense. What self-respecting show business impresario wouldn't sell seats to women and foreigners and freed slaves? A boffo box office, as *Variety* would say, has always been as important as any political or cultural impact a play might have.

One way to get an understanding of how important these festivals were is to look at the money spent on mounting the plays. Demosthenes is said to have complained that the festivals were better financed than the military, and that was no small potatoes. Let's just push pause here and think about that for a moment. Can you imagine living in a world where the military takes a back seat to the arts? What would it be like to live in a society where writers earned a decent living and independent bookstores were subsidized? What if working in the theater was considered heroic sacrifice for the benefit of your country, and musicians and dancers and people with paint splatter in their hair were given priority boarding on flights? Imagine a society where the air force, army, and navy would all compete for National Endowment for the Armed Forces grants. That new bomber? Sorry. Just didn't generate sufficient enthusiasm with our panel. That submarine you requested? We're looking for projects that benefit society. We encourage you to submit next year and suggest you try a seagoing vessel that floats on top of the water. Taxpayers want to see what they're paying for.

And it wasn't just the money that energized the ancient theater world. There was serious prestige to be gained for the writers, actors, musicians, and choragus—essentially a wealthy individual who acted as the patron and producer/director of the chorus, who would bankroll the production and help wrangle the various performers and artisans—from winning the competition.

Who judged the plays and how they judged them are a bit less clear. There were ten official judges, one from each of the original tribes of Athens, chosen by a complicated lottery system, and tampering with the process was punishable by death. But from here it gets murky. Apparently five judges decided the winner. Or, as the second-century CE satirist Lucian of Samosata wrote in his *Harmonides*:

> Public opinion must inevitably follow the
> opinion of the best judges. The public, after
> all, is mainly composed of untutored minds,
> that know not good from bad themselves;
> but when they hear a man praised by the
> great authorities, they take it for granted that
> he is not undeserving of praise, and praise
> him accordingly. It is the same at the games:
> most of the spectators know enough to clap
> or hiss, but the judging is done by some five
> or six persons.[6]

The comedy performances were colorful, loud, and very rude. The spectators could eat, drink, and misbehave. Shouts from the audience could be directed at the actors or the chorus or other patrons in the audience. It was a party. The comic playwrights used this freewheeling atmosphere to their advantage, openly appealing to the audience and judges to award them the prize. There are several instances in Aristophanes's plays where the chorus tries to rally the crowd to influence the judges. It is in these moments, with the crowd provoked, when the comic writers could weaponize their jokes and skewer some of the hypocrisy of the Athenian brand: the folly of sustained war, the disenfranchisement of women, the treatment of the enslaved, and the dangers of demagoguery.

First-century CE writer and rhetorician Quintilian wrote, "Old Comedy is perhaps alone in preserving not only that pure grace of Attic language but also a very potent freedom, and if it is especially good in chasing down vice, it does have a very great deal of power, however, in other areas. For it is grand and elegant and charming . . . there are many authors but especially Aristophanes, Eupolis, and Cratinus."[7]

Aristophanes and his peers would speak out: mocking colleagues and competitors as venomously as they stung other prominent Athenians, deflating egos, bringing the hubristic down to earth, pointing out foibles and depravity, settling personal scores, and igniting new outrages. From the plays and fragments that survived, we know that it was bitingly funny, subversive, and, most of all, self-serving. And sometimes the jokes were just strange, especially in the case of Ariphrades, a man publicly vilified as a practitioner of cunnilingus.

The Case against Ariphrades

In classic Athenian comedies, the agon is the section of the play where a debate or argument happens—the characters take a stand, announce their plans, challenge each other, and variously bicker and quarrel. Aristophanes was brilliant at writing these debates, typically starting with his characters discussing something that seems quite reasonable and then slowly compounding it with more and more absurd accusations and demands until it becomes something else altogether. Which, now that I think of it, is a comedic technique that everyone from Molière to the Marx Brothers to Tina Fey have successfully employed.* Sometimes it's simply the protagonist addressing the audience or chorus with something academics call an "epirrhematic agon," because academics like to make things more complicated.

Let's give Aristophanes his epirrhematic moment. What *did* he say about Ariphrades?

In his play *Knights*, first performed in 424 BCE—and here I'll use Kenneth McLeish's 1979 translation—the chorus of knights have a rolling conversation in the style of a Broadway musical, trading lines and singling out Ariphrades for abuse:

> KNIGHTS: *Ariphrades! That swine!*
> *Who?*
> *Ariphrades.*
> *Never heard of him?*
> *Arignotos' brother. Yes.*
> *Good old Arignotos. One of the best.*
> *So what's wrong with his brother?*

---

*A great example is Abbott and Costello's "Susquehanna Hat Company" routine.

You mean you haven't heard? Some are born vile, some
have vileness thrust upon them—but he invented vileness.
Thrives on it.
Just listen to him playing the flute, then think of the whores
that mouth has blown,
Just imagine that filthy, acrobatic tongue—
And if that doesn't turn your stomach,
Don't imagine you'll ever get a drink from me.[1]

In his translation of the same section of *Knights,* writer Paul Roche decides not to break it up and assigns the whole speech to the leader of the chorus:

LEADER: *There is nothing shameful in showing up the*
shameful.
   It's a good foil for showing up the good,
though I shouldn't have to add
a bad name to a man already bad
or contrast him with a friend of mine who's careful.
   And when it comes to music, I know the bad from good
and can tell an Arignotus from his brother Ariphrades.
They couldn't be more different: Ariphrades is slimy;
But he isn't mere slimy, or I might have passed him by;
He's gone much further and given "slimy" quite a new
dimension with shameful tricks like licking up the dew
in brothels till he sullies
his beard and upsets the hot-stuff ladies . . .
*like a horny Polymnestus or Oenichus his crony.**
   Anyone who doesn't hate the guts of such a man
shan't ever share a cup with me again.[2]

---

* According to Roche: Polymnestus was a seventh-century BCE poet from Colophon. Oenichus was a musician. Which sounds like some of my friends.

In other translations, Ariphrades is "licking the detestable dew in bawdyhouses besmirching his beard, disturbing the ladies' hotpots"[3] or he "pollutes his tongue with shameful pleasures, licking up in his orgies the abominable dew, fouling his beard and tormenting women's privates."[4]

No matter which translation you use, I think we all know what Aristophanes is saying: Ariphrades is going down on flute girls. But proclaiming that it is stomach turning or you should hate the guts of someone who does that feels a bit extreme to my modern sensibility.

In the notes to his 1889 translation of *Knights*, Benjamin Dann Walsh, a fellow of Trinity College of Cambridge University and future first official state entomologist of Illinois, takes Aristophanes at face value: "Although we cannot but esteem our author, for the feeling of disgust which he expresses, at the abominations of which this depraved fellow was guilty, yet it certainly were to be wished, that, while he condemned the offender, he had not spoken quite so plainly out as to the nature of the offence."[5]

I'll try not to make fun of a nineteenth-century bug collector like Walsh; times were different back then and he was, after all, only wishing to save sensitive readers and scholars of the classics from having to imagine what someone might do with his tongue on a clitoris. But I'm personally offended by how judgmental he gets, later referring to Ariphrades as a "besotted debauchee." As someone who has been called a besotted debauchee from time to time, I'm not surprised that a comic writer might have a relationship with alcohol and recreational depravity; there is a long history of writers who liked a drink.* But even modern scholars persist in slandering Ariphrades. For example Robert C. Bartlett, in the notes to his excellent new

---

* From Cratinus to Tennessee Williams, Dorothy Parker to Jean Rhys, Patricia Highsmith to Marguerite Duras, Hunter Thompson to Jay McInerney, with tens of thousands of stops in between.

translations of Aristophanes, name-checks a few characters in the parabasis of *Knights*, writing, "This is followed by the mention of two fellows fully deserving of much censure (Ariphrades and Cleonymus), each licentious in his own way."[6] Really? In our modern epoch oral sex counts as licentiousness? I'm not even sure it qualifies as kinky.

Two years later, Aristophanes went after Ariphrades again in *Wasps*. This time the chorus starts talking about Ariphrades's father, Automenes:

> CHORUS: *Happy Automenes, how we congratulate you! You've begotten sons of the highest artistic skill. First of all a very skilful man, dear to everyone, the supreme lyre-player, on whom delight attends; another, the actor, who's terribly skilful; and then Ariphrades, a long way the most talented of all, who (so his father once swore) without learning it from anybody licked them up every time he went into a brothel.*[7]

In his translation, classicist and notorious wit Moses Hadas puts a slightly more poetic spin on the words: "*Self-inspired he learned, the bawdyhouses among, / How most ingeniously to operate his tongue.*"[8] Which doesn't give credit to the flute girls who might've given him some pointers while he had his face between their legs. It is interesting that Ariphrades is accused of—and credited with—"inventing vileness" that he did "without learning it from anybody."

Do we really think Ariphrades invented cunnilingus? It's hard to say. No one is sure when the Kama Sutra, the ancient Hindu text on lovemaking, was written, but historians place it at around 400 BCE, which means it doesn't predate Ariphrades. And although you'd think that six thousand years of Chinese civilization probably had some form of oral sex going on before the Greeks, Taoism—which advises performing cunnilingus as a way to preserve chi and enhance longevity—also only goes as far back as the fourth century BCE. That's a century later than the Greeks. Which leaves Aristophanes's accusations against Ariphrades as some of the earliest written evidence of the practice we have.

I would love to invent something so important. I'm not talking about a position. There are all kinds of arrangements of limbs and genitals that have different names—doggy style, missionary, cowgirl, reverse cowgirl—but those are all variations on intercourse. Imagine if you patented a new sex act today. What would the licensing and franchise fees be like? Your bank account swelling exponentially as royalties poured in from hundreds of millions of people paying a small fee to perform the sex act you invented. You'd be immensely wealthy and quite possibly beloved, like the person who invented egg cartons. Of course you'd get pirated, there would be counterfeits for sale on the internet, knockoffs coming from China, and slight variations that claim to be original—enough to keep a team of lawyers working full time, enforcing your copyright. But as far as we know, Ariphrades made no claim on cunnilingus; if he did invent it, he put it up on Creative Commons as shareware.

Did he, as Aristophanes claimed, acquire the skill on his own? I don't know what the sex ed classes were like in the ancient gymnasiums, but there were certainly guides to sex: a woman named Philaenis of Samos is credited, and subsequently discredited by some scholars, with writing an early sex manual. But for Aristophanes to publicly acknowledge Ariphrades for his self-taught skills was not a compliment, it was a public pronouncement that the rival satirist was not up to the standards of Athenian manhood. Aristotle said, "The male is by nature superior and the female inferior . . . the one rules and the other is ruled."[9] To an upstanding Athenian male of the time, Ariphrades's actions would have been problematic at the least.

The third instance of Aristophanes talking smack about Ariphrades is really just a throwaway line in the play *Peace* from 421 BCE, as two characters discuss how to deliver a maiden to her betrothed.

> SERVANT: *Who! Ariphrades: he wants her brought his way.*
> TRYGAEUS: *No: I can't bear his dirty, sloppy way.*[10]

It's a minor slap, more in line with what Chris Rock said about R. Kelly eating ass* than a major callout. You can detect a hint of exhaustion, as if Aristophanes didn't really want to go there but couldn't resist, like he was trying to get the last word in.

Thirty years later in *Assemblywomen*—a raunchy comedy about a kind of collective society that enforces sexual equality for the old and unattractive—he again singles Ariphrades out, this time with a single line: "*Stop gabbing, Ariphrades! Come, sit down*"[11] As if Ariphrades has arrived late, wiping excess secretions from his beard and causing a disturbance.

And there's another mention in an undated, untitled play where the line reads: "*I'm afraid that Ariphrades will eat away our business for us!*"[12] I can only imagine that this is a conversation between two men opening a brothel. Mentioning this fragment in an article entitled "How to Avoid Being a *Komodoumenos*," historian Alan H. Sommerstein writes, "The Aristophanic status of this fragment is somewhat uncertain, but there is no doubt that it is a fragment of Old Comedy, and its language clearly indicates that the Ariphrades mentioned in it is the alleged cunnilinctor of *Knights*, *Wasps*, and *Peace*."[13]

---

* From Chris Rock's 2004 standup special *Never Scared*: "At one point on the tape, R. Kelly's eating this girl's ass out like it's Puppy Chow. He's in her ass like he's got diabetes and her ass got insulin in it."

Put together, it's a lot. Only eleven of Aristophanes's forty plays have survived, so who knows how many times he hammered away at the same old joke about Ariphrades? Who does that? Imagine being on the receiving end of these tirades. And yet that was where a lot of the humor of Old Comedy came from. Public officials, prominent citizens, rival writers—all kinds of people were subjected to public humiliation on the Athenian stage. There's even a word for it: *komodoumenos*, to be a target of public mockery. These generally had to be well-known individuals, otherwise the joke wouldn't land. As Sommerstein writes, "To ask what sort of people became *komodoumenoi* may be something like asking what made a person well known in fifth-century Athens."

It would be fascinating to hear Ariphrades's riposte. What would he say in his defense? And what jokes would he make about Aristophanes? But all we're left with is a salacious rumor that has somehow persisted, like Catherine the Great fucking her horse.

The Defense of Ariphrades

There is a little hole-in-the-wall place in Athens called Cinque Wine Bar. My wife and I found it by accident while roaming the hip and hustling Psiri neighborhood, a few blocks from Monastiraki Square, the heart of the tourist area near the Acropolis. We were looking for a quiet place to have a glass of wine, which can sometimes be more difficult than you'd think in an area obsessed with selling souvlaki to tourists.

During the day Psiri is a mix of light industry and junk shops that remind me of Canal Street in New York City during the '80s. Vendors stack dusty books, battered electrical parts, used hardware, clothing, tchotchkes, old cooking pots, power tools, burner phones—basically anything and everything you don't really want or need—onto the sidewalk and spilling out into streets. It is difficult to navigate during the day and, unless you're looking for a pair of Soviet-era jumper cables or an outdated math textbook in German, is an area I avoid. However, at night it transforms; the junk is cleared away, and hip restaurants and bars spring to life. It's just as chaotic, but a completely different vibe.

Cinque is tucked away from the main bustle on a little side street. It's a quiet and friendly bar that serves only Greek wines by small vintners, plates of local cheese, and homemade chutneys. In other words, it is my kind of place. The owners, Grigoris and Evangelia, are fanatical about Greek wine and gave me a splash-by-splash tour of the oenological output of the entire country. Grigoris, or Greg, is an exuberant man who likes to tell stories. His English is limited—but much better than my nonexistent Greek—so that Evangelia was pulled into the conversation to act as his good-natured but slightly put-upon translator and the straight (wo)man to his jokes. They are excellent company and have a nose for delicious wines.

Much like Alcibiades at the symposium, I got plastered.

Wine has a way of forging friendships, and on subsequent visits, after a glass or two, I began telling them about my interest in Ariphrades. It turned out that Evangelia has a sister who studies ancient Greek. She called her sister and, after a few minutes, came back with a translation of the name.

Ari = "crude" or "rude."

Phrades = "speaking."

According to Evangelia's sister, the name signifies someone who is rude or, perhaps, someone who uses his tongue in a crude way. Did it mean he was salty? The Lenny Bruce of the Agora? Or was it the other way he used his tongue? I wasn't quite convinced. It seemed too on the nose, you know? Like his reputation was coloring how people translated his name. But besides that, what parents name their kid Crude Talker? It just didn't seem like something Automenes would do. So I checked the Eulexis-web lemmatiser* for ancient Greek texts and *ari* turned up as a prefix, "an inseparable particle, marking an idea of strength, of superiority." Google Translate turns Ariphrades into "Mars Phrases," which sounds like a great name for a new age cat psychologist. I found the contradictions funny, and, like a lot of things about ancient Athens, the more you investigate, the less you know.

I asked Mary Norris, author of the excellent travelogue/language acquisition memoir *Greek to Me*[1] if she had an idea what his name might mean. She told me that *aristo* means "best," as in "aristocracy," and hazarded a guess that "Aristophanes means something like 'he appears the best.'" She added,

---

* I'd never heard of it before either, but to quote Wikipedia: "Lemmatisation (or lemmatization) in linguistics is the process of grouping together the inflected forms of a word so they can be analysed as a single item, identified by the word's lemma, or dictionary form."

"I am not sure if *ari* means 'superior' without the *stǫ*. Anyway, etymology of names is dangerous territory." Personally, I like a frisson of danger when I'm trying to do research.

If you've read her charming memoir of being a copy editor, *Between You & Me: Confessions of a Comma Queen*,[2] you'll know that she likes precision. She asked James Romm, the James H. Ottaway Jr. Professor of Classics at Bard College and author of several books on the ancient world, what he made of Ariphrades's name.

James replied immediately: "As to Ariphrades: the meaning is 'very wise,' to go by the lexicon. You're right that *ari-* is connected to *aristos* but does not convey 'best' so much as 'very.' The adjective *phradês* simply means 'wise.'"

That seems more like it. Not to say that Ariphrades was very wise, but it feels like a name parents might give their child.

In ancient Greek it looks like this: Ἀριφράδης.

Apart from the harangues in Aristophanes's plays, the most telling reference to Ariphrades is in Aristotle's *Poetics*, a collection of essays on literary theory that might be the first known *Writing for Dummies*. Circa 335 BCE, Aristotle wrote, "Again, Ariphrades satirised the tragedians for using phrases which no one would ever speak in ordinary discourse."

There's a break in the translation noted by the symbol [. . .], which signals an omission of some quotations "whose relative points cannot be successfully rendered into English."

Aristotle continues: "But he failed to realise that it is just because of their absence from ordinary language that all such things produce a heightened effect in poetic diction."[3]

The Loeb Classical Library, a multivolume series of works written in ancient Greek and Latin, takes a crack at a translation of the same brief mention:

> Ariphrades would make fun of the tragic
> poets because they employed the sort of
> language that no one would ever use in
> conversation, such as "the halls from out"
> (instead of "from the halls") and "of thee"
> and "and I him" and "Achilles concerning"
> (instead of "concerning Achilles") and other
> such expressions. Because they are not present
> in ordinary conversation, these sorts of
> things produce an unusual effect in speech,
> but Ariphrades did not realise this.[4]

I don't think Aristotle got the joke. Or, if he did, it hit a little too close to home. Because there is a long history in the comedic arts, and theater in particular, of mocking elites: the know-it-alls, the chewers of scenery, the orators who are egregiously sesquipedalian. That's how comedy works. We like to see people who think highly of themselves fall into a pile of shit. It's the other shoe dropping, the pratfall, and the comeuppance that makes us laugh. Is there anything funnier than deflating a pretentious blowhard?

Perhaps Ariphrades was making a barbed political point, extending his middle finger to poetic pretentiousness and highborn aristocratic ways, revealing the renown poets of the day to be part of a self-aggrandizing echo chamber of ego inflation, logrolling, and back patting. Kind of like what Marcel Duchamp had in mind when he signed a urinal "R. Mutt" and put it in an art museum.

It is undeniable that Aristotle's *Poetics* is a formidable piece of writing. He was one of the first philosophers to look at how narrative structure works and to unpack the emotional ways that stories—especially the catharsis of tragedy—affect us. Although it doesn't appear he had much of a sense of humor. He believed that tragedy was the superior art, as it deals with issues of life, death, honor, and virtue in a serious way, where comedy is an inferior form concerning itself with the less virtuous, the scofflaws and scoundrels, the con artists and cowards, and focuses on human weaknesses. This kind of drama versus comedy snobbery is nothing new. For reasons that are unclear to me, comedy has always been treated as the slightly troublesome younger sibling. Just look at the films honored at award ceremonies or the books that win the Pulitzer Prize. It is rare to find an out-and-out comedy in the pantheon of Western civilization.* It may be self-serving of me to say so, but I think we ignore comedy at our peril. People who say laughs are cheap have never tried writing comedy, they have never paid full price.

Poetics was written almost ninety years after the golden age of Old Comedy; the playwrights like Ariphrades and Aristophanes who once enthralled Athens had died before Aristotle was born. What that means is that the comic plays of Ariphrades either had survived on papyrus or were still being performed almost one hundred years after they were written. Ariphrades must have been famous, or infamous, enough that an important scholar like Aristotle would include him in his *Poetics* along with other well-known writers from the same period like Euripides, Aeschylus, and Cleophon.**

Aristotle references Ariphrades in much the same way we might cite *Smokey and the Bandit* when discussing the important films of 1977. While it might not be high art—I can't really imagine Aristotle enjoying it—*Smokey and the Bandit* was the second-highest-grossing film that year. Ariphrades's work might not ascend to the poetic height of the great tragedians, but the locals needed a laugh. Which makes me think that the crude-speaking, muff-diving comic playwright might have

---

* Notable exceptions include Paul Beatty's *The Sellout* and John Kennedy Toole's *A Confederacy of Dunces.*
** Another writer whose work has not survived.

been in on the joke himself. Perhaps that's what made him popular with the demos, the common people.

We don't know much about Ariphrades's family life or background. In the Loeb Classical Library entry about Ariphrades, it says, "The name is rare at Athens, at this or at any other period, and is known principally for one of Aristophanes' targets." The other information comes from Aristophanes's plays, which we've already looked at. All we know about his father is that he was named Automenes. We know Ariphrades had a brother, Arignotus, who was a musician and another who was an actor. He was, apparently, from a family that put an importance on arts education.

In his book *Fathers and Sons in Athens: Ideology and Society in the Era of the Peloponnesian War*, historian Barry S. Strauss writes,

> Aristophanes takes the low road by emphasizing Automenes' role in begetting these sons with their peculiar talents and by having him swear that Ariphrades acquired his talent "without any teaching from anyone"—in other words, like son, like father. Comic exaggeration, but it probably paints a realistic picture of Athenian fathers calling their sons "chips off the old block." Ariphrades may have been a comic poet, and perhaps Automenes (of whom nothing is known) really did brag about his natural *poetic* skill.[5]

Other than being from a family in show business, we can assume that Ariphrades lived the relatively straightforward and privileged life of an Athenian citizen.

When young men turned eighteen they took the Ephebic Oath, in which they swore not to dishonor their city or abandon a comrade and to honor the gods of their fathers, etcetera. A lot like the Boy Scout oath, it was essentially a promise to obey the rules of the society without asking a lot of questions. As classical scholar Joseph Roisman says in his book *The Rhetoric of Manhood,* masculinity in Athens was defined as being "willing to rank public interest over personal needs, courageous in war and politics, competitive within approved boundaries." It goes on for a bit, extolling citizens to be "truthful, hardworking, careful, practical, intelligent, guided by reason," and, in my favorite part, requires that a young Athenian should be "able to control his appetites."[6]

Protecting your family honor and guarding against embarrassment was a big deal for Athenians, and the threat of shaming someone was used to enforce the norms of the day. As Demosthenes said, "Ordinary men are deterred from wrongdoing by their fear of shame and public opinion; and wicked men are corrected by punishment."[7] In his plays, Aristophanes refers to Ariphrades as "wicked" for performing cunnilingus. In fifth-century BCE Athens, this would be seen as submitting to women, and that could be construed as a betrayal of the Athenian ideals.

I find it strange that the author of *Lysistrata*—a play about the women of Athens going on a sex strike until the Peloponnesian War is ended—would be such a prude. Like most great comedy, there is always a political nucleus embedded in the joke. At the time, the aristocracy was under attack from the rampant populism on the streets—led by Kleon and others— and shaming Ariphrades was a way to remind the public that the male citizens were in charge and anyone who stepped outside the lines of proud Athenian manhood, even by pleasuring flute girls, deserved reproach. That Ariphrades seemed to own his actions—because why else would Aristophanes continue to attack him?—would've been seen as a big fuck you to the noble families.

We can hear echoes of the ancient patriarchy nowadays in the handwringing of conservatives over gay marriage; to quote Bryan Fischer of the American Family Association, "the homosexual agenda" is "the greatest immediate threat to every freedom and right that is enshrined in the First Amendment."[8] Sex that questions what it means to be a man in society threatens the status quo, causing the patriarchy to panic. Just look at the bizarre hullabaloo over transgender rights. Are conservative Americans really so terrified that they might find themselves urinating next to someone who may or may not be of some indeterminate sex that they have to pass laws against it? Have they never been to Europe? Are they really obsessed with bathrooms, or are they, like the ruling aristocracy of Athens, trying to disempower people who don't fit their idea of American manhood?

These ancient comedies had political bite. They influenced public opinion; they affected how a person was received and if he was respected in society. A joke had the potential to ruin you or worse. A well-known orator named Hyperbolus—yes, that's where we get the word—was often the target of satire on the Athenian stage; he was mocked for being dumb, corrupt, a pervert, and, in a nod to contemporary birther scandals, a bastard. And not just by Aristophanes. Apparently Hyperbolus was also ridiculed by Eupolis, a leading writer of Old Comedy. Some historians believe the constant ridicule was the cause of his ostracism and subsequent murder.

With political change in the air—the aristocracy under attack from a burgeoning populism gaining power in the assembly—the comic stage, which had always had a bias toward the traditional hierarchy in Athens, turned out to be an excellent vehicle to take potshots at, humiliate, and mock the leaders of the new populist movement. Which is not to say that Aristophanes and Eupolis were right-wingers, although some scholars believe they were—but a successful comedian will always tailor material to the audience. A sexually forthright comedian like Nikki Glaser might kill at a club in New York but find her jokes falling flat at a comedy show in Branson, Missouri, for the same reason Christian comedian Pastor Ted Cunningham's clean comedy might flop on the Sunset Strip. There is a confirmation bias between an audience and a comedian. If Ariphrades was more of a man of the street, a voice for the demos, then his public humiliation on the stages of Athens might very well have been an effort to keep the aristocracy in power.

I'm not really much of a conspiracy theorist; I don't think 9/11 was an inside job or that the Illuminati secretly run the World Bank. And yet I have a suspicion that something's not right.

In *The Swerve: How the World Became Modern*, author Stephen Greenblatt explores the history behind Roman poet Lucretius's *On the Nature of Things*—an interpretation of the writings of Epicurus that promotes reason, science, and the pursuit of pleasure over obedience to any deity. Greenblatt finds enough evidence to allow him to speculate that the early Catholic Church had reason to suppress Lucretius's document and that its eventual discovery in the fifteenth century inspired the Renaissance.[9] Greenblatt won a National Book Award and a Pulitzer Prize for his work, but contemporary Christian scholars dumped all over it, giving *The Swerve* scathing reviews, which, to my mind, kinda proved his point.

There is a connection between Ariphrades, Epicurus, and Lucretius. They all promoted—or were accused of promoting—a kind of egalitarian pleasure seeking that would fly in the face of the strict rules of organized religion and an entrenched patriarchy. But maybe it goes deeper. It wasn't just Ariphrades whose work disappeared. With the exception of Aristophanes, the other great comic writers of the golden era of Old Comedy—

Cratinus, Eupolis, Crates, Aristomenes, Philonides, the list goes on—also had their work vanish. These were comedies that, from what we can tell by the fragments, were sexually risqué and politically outspoken. Was there some kind of organized destruction of the old comedies? Some humorless mage in a castle who demanded comedy vanquished from history? Maybe Aristophanes is the sole survivor simply because someone took it upon himself to preserve his plays.

Amazonon Street

The taxi met us at the ferry terminal in Piraeus, the driver managing to pick us out of the crowd of island hoppers disembarking from a massive ferry into a crowded parking lot. How he picked me out of a crowd using the picture from my WhatsApp profile I don't know. Either I am distinctive looking or he should be a detective, but he didn't hesitate. We loaded up his cab and began the drive into Athens. It was late, maybe ten at night, so traffic was light and the city was dark. My wife, Diana,* and I were being dropped off at an Airbnb while our friends were staying at a hotel.

The driver cruised down Pireos—it wasn't long before the Acropolis came into view— then turned onto Plateon and into the neighborhood where the Airbnb was. We slowed as the road narrowed and streetlights became unreliable. It was dark, but it was hard to miss the collapsed buildings, the dilapidated streets, the broken sidewalks, and the fact that every wall was splattered with street art and graffiti—the streets greeting us with the distressed embrace of urban blight. Unlike other cities I've been in, where an area like this would be desolate, the streets were alive; it seemed like there was a bar or taverna on every corner packed with people, every table full, the insides overflowing, with clusters of young Athenians drinking beer in the street, smoking joints on corners, going walkabout in the alleys. We rolled past a partially demolished building where the empty courtyard had been converted into an open-air

---

*I'd like to take a moment and give a shout-out to my wife. She is an excellent travel companion and research assistant: easygoing, enthusiastic, and fearless. She has braved a book signing at a nudist resort, climbed up the rigging of a sailing ship as it was crossing the Dardanelles, eaten very spicy food in Cuzco, and managed to find an espresso bar in Constanta, Romania, when we really needed a coffee. She is game for whatever is next and never leaves an unfinished bottle of wine on the table.

speakeasy with a crowded bar and a sound system pumping out chillwave techno. One of our friends said, "Are you sure this is the right address?" We nodded. We had been here before and we couldn't wait to get out of the cab and go get a drink.

It's easy to see why someone who didn't know the scene might think we were being dropped into some kind of no-go zone for tourists, the kind of area Fox News warns you about, but we knew the street art here was mostly political and anti-fascist—we were friends with a few of the artists—and that the tavernas and bars served some of the best food in Athens. Metaxourgeio was our secret, even if it is impossible to pronounce.

The neighborhood has experienced the traditional trajectory of cool neighborhoods: formerly an industrial area with a predominantly immigrant population; then overrun by junkies and drug dealers; abandoned for a time; now home to artists and people looking for affordable housing. It reminds me of Brooklyn before it was hot, or maybe SoHo in the late '70s, or the Arts District in Los Angeles in the '80s—basically any urban area, pre-gentrification, where bombed-out buildings, modern apartments, cafés, tavernas, and abundant street life converge in dynamic and interesting ways. We discovered it during a street art tour two years before. It was one of those places where Diana and I looked at each other and said, "We could live here."

When I tell people that I love Athens, how it is one of the few cities in the world where I would like to live, they invariably wrinkle their noses and start saying things like, "What about the crime? The traffic? The horrible pollution?" As if these things don't exist in every big city. I've been to a lot of places and I have to tell you, Athens is fucking amazing. Which is not to say it's some idealized, perfect urban place. It has the same multitude of problems any major urban area can have. But I dig it. I can only guess the bad rap comes from disgruntled tourists who expect every part of the city to be as magnificent as the Acropolis. It's not a fair comparison—there aren't many buildings in the world as magnificent as the Parthenon. I have friends who come to Athens and stay at fancy hotels on the beach outside of the city. They take a cab to see a couple of sights and then bounce to the airport or hop on a ferry to the islands. It's their loss. Away from the tourist sector, Athens is dynamic, alive and fascinating and funky.

Outside our Airbnb we were greeted by graffiti stenciled on a building that read:

(*Photograph courtesy of the author*)

It's perhaps hypocritical to agree with a sign telling you to fuck off, but that is exactly what I would tell an Airbnb tourist if I wasn't, you know, an Airbnb tourist. For whatever reason, I felt oddly comforted by it. Much like Henry Miller writing about Athens in *The Colossus of Maroussi,* the freewheeling travelogue of his adventures in Greece in 1939: "I had the strange feeling of being at home, of being in a spot so familiar, so altogether like home should be that from looking at it with such intense adoration it had become a new and strange place."[1]

Athens has a long history of being open and welcoming to immigrants and visitors, and classical Athens was where that began. There were restrictions, naturally—the citizens of Athens didn't want to cede voting rights or land ownership to noncitizens—but otherwise newcomers, called "metics," were welcome and many of them became important members of society. For example Aristotle and Diogenes the Cynic were metics, as was noted speechwriter-for-hire Lysias and the philosopher Protagoras. There were other, less famous metics, people who came to the city for much the same reason people have always come to cities—displaced by war, drought, or famine or just looking for the opportunity to improve their lives. In the fifth century BCE, Athens was an economic power, a place where jobs could be had and money could be made.

What a difference a couple thousand years make. In 2021 Athens and Greece are still struggling to recover from a program of economic austerity imposed on them by the European Union and the European Central Bank after the 2008 worldwide financial collapse. In 2018 Mário Centeno, head of the Eurogroup, trumpeted, "Greece joins Ireland, Spain, Cyprus and my own country Portugal, in the ranks of euro area countries that turned around their economies and once again stand on their own feet. A success story of programme implementation."[2]

That is a steaming pile of absolute bullshit, presented as if the Eurogroup's abject cruelty did the Greek people a favor. As *The World* public radio program reported at the time of Centeno's announcement:

> Greeks are still reeling from heavy pension cuts, tax hikes and troubling levels of unemployment, (which at 20 percent remain the highest in the Eurozone despite having dropped in recent years). Years and years of crippling austerity measures have shrunk

Greece's economy by a quarter, prompting
hundreds of thousands of young people to
emigrate and pushing nearly half the country's
elderly below the poverty line.[3]

If that's a "success story," what would a failure look like?

A University of Washington study funded by the Bill and Melinda Gates Foundation found that "from 2010 to 2016, Greece was faced with a five-times greater rate of annual all-cause mortality increase and a more modest increase in non-fatal health loss compared with pre-austerity."[4] This includes deaths due to suicide, depression, and alcohol and drug abuse, all part of what happens when a population finds their livelihood, security, and dignity stripped from them by a corrupt banking system. A five times greater rate of death—can you imagine? That's a humanitarian crisis, not a debt-repayment program. Which makes the moralizing of European bureaucrats especially odious.

The crisis is typically framed as if the Greeks brought it upon themselves. Former Greek finance minister Yanis Varoufakis defined "austerity" in his book *Adults in the Room*: "Austerity is a morality play pressed into the service of legitimizing cynical wealth transfers from the have-nots to the haves during times of crisis, in which debtors are sinners who must be made to pay for their misdeeds."[5]

Like lots of cities that emerge from hardship—Barcelona after Franco, Berlin after the fall of the wall—sometimes you get a burst of creative energy. When society receives a shock, when your hopes and dreams and plans get fucked over by a situation out of your control, then it's time to make new ones. As boxer Mike Tyson so eloquently said, "Everybody has a plan until they get punched in the mouth." Sometimes the only reasonable response is to pack up and go. Beginning in 2010, almost half a million young Greeks immigrated to other countries. An article in the *Financial Times* in 2018 stated that more than two-thirds of the émigrés were university graduates or people with postgraduate degrees.[6] It was an epic brain drain, with tens of thousands of doctors and engineers leaving for European Union countries like the Netherlands, Belgium, and Germany. At one point the Australian embassy held a job fair to entice highly educated Greeks to move down under. For the ones who stayed, many of the available jobs were in the service and tourism industries.

All this is nothing new for Athenians. The city was sacked by the Persians in 480 BCE, besieged by the Macedonians and a couple of Roman armies over the next hundred or so years, sacked again by Germanic barbarians in 267 CE, and then overrun by the Ottomans. Austerity is just another kind of siege by barbarians from the north.

Artemis in Exarchia (*photograph courtesy of the author*).

The Exarchia neighborhood near the University of Athens probably best represents the dynamics of the current crisis. In 2008 an argument between two police officers and a group of teenagers resulted in one of the policemen shooting and killing a fifteen-year-old student named Alexander Grigoropoulos. This incident lit the fuse of pent-up frustration caused by the financial crisis and the imposition of austerity. Exarchia exploded. As you might expect when you have an entire population who feel they're being fucked over, protests, rioting, and running street battles with the police ensued. Demonstrations against austerity popped up in other cities and there was a general sense of unrest throughout Greece.

Talking to people about it reminds me of my experiences during the Brixton riots of 1981, the Los Angeles uprising of 1992,[*] and the Black Lives Matter protests that took place all across the United States in the summer of 2020, when the hopeful energy of standing up for justice is met with the fear that the police will use increasingly violent measures to restore the status quo. Typically that's what happens. The police crack down, the media stop covering it, the anger fizzles out or is directed elsewhere, and nothing much changes. Just look at the lip service politicians paid to Black Lives Matter protesters. They said all the right things—maybe they even meant it when they said it— but when the legislation is ultimately enacted, it's weak sauce, diluted by the police union and other special interests until it is basically the same thing as before, except the police aren't allowed to choke you to death. People are resistant to change, the status quo does not want to be moved. It takes a change of consciousness to change the way things exist, and even then it's never easy.

It didn't happen that way in Exarchia. Not exactly. On my first visit to the neighborhood in 2016, I was struck by the multiple

---

[*] Weird to think I have been in both Brixton and Los Angeles when major rioting occurred.

police checkpoints I passed on my way in. Once I was inside, there were no police to be seen along the quiet, tree-lined streets or in any of the tavernas that line the pleasant square. Aside from the husk of a burned-out automobile and some broken glass, there were no signs of any uprising, no whiff of tear gas; the whole place was pretty chill. Which makes sense, because from the students' point of view, the police were forced out; from the cops' point of view, the anarchists and troublemakers were kept in. If a demonstration tried to burst out of the confines of the neighborhood, there were squads of riot police waiting.

For the last ten years or so a kind of equilibrium had been achieved, a working standoff that suited both sides. And in a refreshing change from what typically happens in the United States when police kill an unarmed man, the Greek policeman was sentenced to life in prison for "homicide with direct intention to cause harm."

In many ways Exarchia is like any neighborhood around a major university: there are bars and head shops, coffee shops and tavernas, bookstores, guitar stores, boutiques selling vintage clothing, and the best-named record store in the world, Bowel of Noise. And like Metaxourgeio, every surface is covered by street art—some of it breathtakingly beautiful, much of it political. Slapped next to the art are thick layers of posters for rock shows, plays, demonstrations, lectures, and protests of all kinds. It is layers of information and images, built up for years, strata of protest and outrage, community organizing and anarchy. Some people say it's "visual noise" or "eye pollution," and I will be the first to admit that when "Sleepy" and "Stonker" tag the wall of my house in Los Angeles, I'm not happy about it, but those are gang tags, teenagers trying to claim some street cred. I know I sound like a hypocrite, but it's different in Athens. It's not about claiming territory, it is public discourse through art, a return to the beginnings of democracy, in a city where citizens have publicly voiced their thoughts and feelings for thousands of years.

The graffiti and art are all over the university, which surprised me. And when I told an Athenian friend this would never happen at an American campus, he was shocked. He said, "It's a public space. The people own the walls and should be allowed to express themselves."

Antifa in Exarchia (*photograph courtesy of the author*).

From my tourist point of view, I feel an undeniable energy in the streets of Metaxourgeio and Exarchia, something that portends a shift in fortunes for Athens. But maybe that's just me. I asked urban geographer and longtime Exarchia resident George Papamattheakis what he thought about the current situation. George is a student at the Harokopio University of Athens, where he's working on a postgraduate degree in applied social geography. He has also studied in Moscow, at the Strelka

Institute for Media, Architecture and Design. George is one of those guys who seems to know everyone, at least everyone in his neighborhood. Perhaps that's because he's good-looking and friendly, or maybe because he rocks one of the best mustaches this side of Freddie Mercury.

George and his girlfriend, Jenny, agreed to meet Diana and me at Seychelles, an excellent bistro in Metaxourgeio. They were leaving the next morning for their summer vacation, and Jenny brought her fully loaded backpack into the restaurant as if she were preparing to camp out. Now that I think of it, that's not a bad idea. The restaurant is fantastic. Why leave?

We talked a lot that night—mostly about the delicious wine, a Xinomavro rosé, and their impending trip to Naxos—but also about what was happening in the city. I told George that the U.S. embassy in Athens had issued a warning about Exarchia. Americans were advised to avoid it.

George rubbed his eyes. "I didn't know that."

I laughed. "It's probably why I like the place. What would you say to someone who is considering going to Exarchia?"

"Exarchia is being depicted in the media as the ghetto of Athens, so maybe this is why the American embassy put out this warning. In my opinion, it's nothing like that. I would say that it's an open neighborhood. Up until last year, I would also say that it's safe. I would never advise people not to walk here at night. On the contrary, people coming here to settle as students, even younger girls, I would say that there's no problem in you walking around late at night, coming back home, all of these things. But there is—in the past year, especially, there has been a surge in microcriminality, like thefts, things like that."

I have never heard the expression "microcriminality," but having lost my sunglasses to a pickpocket in Monastiraki Square, I can attest to how annoying it can be. Yet it might be a small indignity to suffer if it meant that you could be free of police harassment, especially for refugees and people of color.

Or perhaps I'm just projecting the abysmal state of policing currently on display in the United States. There's a reason there's a movement toward defunding or reallocating police budgets by groups like Black Lives Matter. When the police no longer serve the community that pays their salaries, does it make sense to have a police department? I'm curious, because I think it might be an answer to a host of problems. I asked George, "What's it like to live in an area without police? How is the neighborhood organized?"

"Well, it's technically still under the municipality, right? So it's not self-organized at the neighborhood level. There is some kind of assembly of people, but this doesn't really have authority. They're just organizing public events, some green markets, things like that. But there are different kinds of collectives running in Exarchia. Some of them are very straightforwardly political, like the anarchists, or the autonomists, or the communist anarchy, so they have some very specific direction. For example, the other well-known assembly, which is Rouvikonas, is an anarchist collective that have a very specific political direction that they are pursuing."

Which, when you think about it, is totally in keeping with how early Athenians developed democracy. People got together and discussed ways of organizing the city and living their lives. That doesn't mean there wasn't a version of law enforcement in ancient Athens; the Scythian archers[*] performed that duty, patrolling the streets and arresting people whom the council deemed worthy of detention. And not everyone is happy with Exarchia's experiment in self-governance. In the summer of 2019, a new and conservative mayor, Kostas Bakoyannis, a member of the center-right New Democracy party, took office and vowed to "reclaim Exarchia."

---

[*] That there isn't a band with this name is baffling.

George sighed. "It's part of this whole ghetto narrative, how we're going to clean up Exarchia, how we're going to make Exarchia safer. And then open up a new metro station right in the square of Exarchia. At the same time, a lot of investors from abroad are buying property in Athens, especially Chinese capital investors, who are buying a lot of real estate in Exarchia."

Back in Metaxourgeio, I sat on the balcony of the Amazonon Street apartment in the shade of a tree. More than thirty feet tall, the tree rose out of the sidewalk and provided a canopy over the balcony. It was like having a tree house connected to the apartment. I could sit out there, drink a glass of wine, and eat olives as the sounds of the neighborhood filtered in: the dull thud of techno coming from the top of the block, the clatter of dishes in a taverna at the other end, the buzz of Vespas, the murmur of conversation. The sun might be hot, but the tree provided shade. It was, as you might imagine, very pleasant. It was easy to see why Epicurus built his garden nearby.

In the Athens of Ariphrades's time, Metaxourgeio would've been olive groves or small farms. Students on their way to Plato's Academy would exit through the Dipylon gate in the Kerameikos and walk along a road that passed through the cemetery outside the city walls, an area lined with statuary tributes to fallen war heroes, beloved spouses, and important citizens. You can still see the remnants of this in the Kerameikos museum, a large open area littered with grandiose funerary monuments and the ruins of the ancient city walls. That road cut through the heart of where I was now sitting. I wish I could say that I heard ancient voices or felt some kind of ethereal presence in the streets of Metaxourgeio, but that wouldn't be true. Maybe it's too old; maybe the spirits have moved on. But people have been walking past this spot for thousands of years, talking about the weather, food, sex, war, philosophy—whatever was on their minds, all the things we talk about today; they gossiped, they had heart-to-hearts, they made jokes.

Humor was an important part of their lives, and the ancient comic playwrights and poets had the license to be funny, to mock and satirize, to point out the absurd, to take the trials and tribulations and suffering of life and use it as grist for a laugh. It was the news and editorial pages of the day, the writers responding to current events, commenting on them, and influencing public opinion. The jokes weren't meant to last millennia; they were ephemeral, the hot takes of their day.

I feel real gratitude for those scribes and for the continuum of irreverent writers and comedic comrades in arms who followed them. Musicians always talk about how the Beach Boys influenced the Beatles, who in turn influenced the Beach Boys, or the bluesmen who influenced the Rolling Stones, who then influenced the Clash, who influenced the Pixies, and so on. That kind of influence exists with writers too. We're predominantly readers, so what we read affects what and how we write. Aristophanes and other Greek satirists influenced Roman writers like Lucian and Martial, who inspired Molière, who influenced Joe Orton, who influenced Larry David, who influenced Abbi Jacobson and Ilana Glazer. It's the same with fiction and nonfiction, and it's especially true for people writing with humorous intent. You can draw a line from Mary Roach and Marian Keyes, David Sedaris and Paul Beatty, through Kingsley Amis and Graham Greene, Machado de Assis and Laurence Sterne, all the way back to the Greeks. Writing is an ongoing conversation between writers running all the way back to ancient Athens. It may not look like there's a direct connection, but you can feel it, especially when you read the work of ancient Athenian writers; they don't seem that distant.

Maybe it was the wine and the sharp Athens sunlight filtering through the tree, but out on that balcony I felt like I was a part of the conversation. I'm not saying that my work is at the same level as those people—many of whom I consider geniuses—and there are lots of names I've left out; but I feel lucky to be a tiny part of it.* Somehow being in Athens made me feel connected.

Becoming a writer was not something I planned. Like almost everything I've done, for better or worse, I fell into it. I can't even say I'm self-taught; I learned by reading—as much and as widely as I possibly could—and scribbling weird ideas for my own amusement. I did take a creative writing class once, in my freshman year of college. I don't remember much about it. I definitely don't remember any of the notes the professor might've given about the Richard Brautigan–influenced drivel I was churning out at the time. But I distinctly remember going to the typewriter room at the library and typing a story onto special mimeograph paper so that it could be copied and handed out to the class. And I'll never forget a student in the class who wrote erotica, like an undergraduate Anaïs Nin, presenting short stories about encounters with ghosts or the spirit world that were sexually explicit. She would often wear a diaphanous peasant blouse as she read these stories to the class. To this day, I find the smell of mimeograph ink kind of a turn-on.

It was almost ten years later that I started to take the idea of writing seriously. I had been initially inspired by reading Patricia Highsmith—and seeing the movies made from her Ripley novels like *The American Friend*—but I had never found a way to successfully combine humor with crime fiction and still have it feel authentic and political. Then a friend took me to see a couple of plays by British playwright Joe Orton and they blew my mind. It wasn't just the irreverence, the sly humor,

---

* Please note that, for the most part, I am talking about Eurocentric writers here. Comedy is a fundamental part of the human makeup and there are equally funny writers, playwrights, and poets in every culture around the world.

or the energy and anarchy of *Loot* and *Entertaining Mr. Sloane* that changed the way I thought about writing; it was the way Orton articulated his worldview. It wasn't cheesy or canned or Catskills stand-up; it was smart and funny theater with a punk rock vibe. And I loved that it was a mix of sexual anarchy and irreverent politics, a kind of drunken phallus procession combined with a hearty middle finger extended toward the conformity and conventionalism of the status quo. It was comedy that made you think. The kind of comedy that asks questions and allows an individual to stand up and say what's on his or her mind—a throwback to the epirrhematic agon—speak truth to the powerful, poke holes in the faulty logic of pedants, mock the small-mindedness of people, and strip away the convenient platitudes of the petit bourgeoisie and reveal something darker underneath. It seemed as if everything was permitted. You could upend the patriarchy and demand justice. As long as you got a laugh.

To paraphrase Che Guevara, the true revolutionary is guided by strong feelings of enjoying a good joke.

A contemporary example might be Jamaican American writer and comedian Sarah Cooper, who creates TikTok clips lip-syncing Donald Trump's unhinged ramblings. She doesn't speak out against him, she doesn't rant, but she uses his own words—and her incredibly funny expressions—not to imitate him but to strip away all the trappings of power, all the skills he uses as a media personality, to reveal what he's saying and the inexplicable way his thoughts unspool. As writer ZZ Packer wrote in the *New York Times,* "What she portrays is not his persona but his affect: the glib overconfidence, the lip curl of dismissiveness, the slow nods of fake understanding."[7] Sarah Cooper destroys Trump. She points out how not only does the emperor have no clothes, but he also appears devoid of any understanding of what it means to be human. And the videos are blisteringly funny. For a thin-skinned and self-obsessed egomaniac like Trump, it must be devastating to know the world is laughing at you. Which might explain why he declared the media service a threat to American interests and said, "As far as TikTok is concerned we're banning them from the United States."[8] Of course he backed off this threat later, but that demonstrates the unique ability of comedy to get under the skin of the powerful.

When I was in graduate school I had an internship on the movie *Lethal Weapon*, starring the great American actor Danny Glover and an up-and-coming Australian named Mel Gibson. I was shadowing the cinematographer, Stephen Goldblatt, so I spent a lot of time on set, watching the camera crew and director work together, learning how scenes are put together. Because actors spend a lot of time standing around, Mel and I struck up a friendly conversation. I made him laugh and he said, "You're funny. You must have a lot of rage." I wouldn't have expressed it this way at the time, but I'd felt *seen*. It unnerved me. I think he must've noticed that and invited me to join him for a Budweiser in his trailer. It was there that he explained he hadn't meant any harm, he just believed that comedy came from an angry place, a psychological wound. I remember drinking my beer and realizing that he was absolutely right, but at that time, I had no idea how the alchemical process of spinning rage and psychological damage into comedy worked.

Comedy can be a coping mechanism for dealing with unpleasant or dangerous emotions, it can be a way to defuse situations, and it also doesn't have to have any serious function, it can be joyful, it can be fun. It speaks to the human condition in a deep and true way. Even if Aristotle writes it off as frivolous and the action of men worse than ourselves. I disagree. We are all worse than ourselves. So we might as well laugh about it.

Sitting on the balcony, in the shade of the tree, drinking a glass of wine and thinking about all these things, about the continuum of writers and readers and thinkers, and the conversation writing has been having with itself through time, I was interrupted by a connection to the real world. I heard a rumble and looked over to see a man in a cherry picker rising from the street, suddenly level with the balcony. He was wearing the hard hat and bright yellow safety vest of someone who had the authority to do whatever he was about to do. He flashed me a sheepish smile, fired up his chain saw, and began cutting the tree down.

I shouted, "I don't need a fucking metaphor." But he didn't understand English and I couldn't communicate in Greek, and so the tree was dismantled, branch by branch. I wish I could say I strode out into the street and battled the workmen like a true California tree hugger, but I didn't. I was a guest in their city, an Airbnb tourist who had been told to fuck off.

As I watched the tree being butchered—the cool shade of the leaves falling away and the sun suddenly too hot, too bright—I thought about all the writers, comic and otherwise, whose work has been lost over time. Names I had come across in my research, writers like Phrynichus, Myrtilus, Ameipsias, Lysippus, Nicophon, and, of course, Ariphrades. I can imagine that these writers all had a lot of anger. If the fragments that survived are any indication, these were writers who lampooned the comfortable, explored sexual politics, mocked the imperial war machine, and basically made jokes at the expense of anyone and everyone who they felt deserved it. In a word, they *raged*. Maybe that's why they've now become pruned from literary history. It makes me wonder if anyone's work will be around in two thousand years. With our reliance on digital archives, are we just one solar flare away from having our entire written history obliterated?

The Buddha said, "Ardently do today what must be done. Who knows? Tomorrow, death comes."[9] Which is cheery. But the point is well taken. Nothing lasts forever. Try to enjoy the moment before the chain saw comes out. This is why what writers do is vital. We examine our wounds and we rage; we let our curiosity off leash and dive into the unknown and illuminate our humanness—the comedy and tragedy of existence, the inescapable presence of death—to give a voice to thoughts and feelings in a specific place and time and feel the interconnection between everything around us and everyone who came before us and everyone who will come after. The act of writing opens a conversation with the past and the present. And it gives us the opportunity to thumb our noses, make farting sounds, and do anything that humanizes a world that is increasingly dehumanizing and algorithmic. That's meaningful. Even if the work doesn't get published. Even if it gets lost.

After the tree was chopped into bits and hauled away, we learned that a man who lived across the street had paid for its removal over the protests of the other neighbors. It wasn't even his tree, but he liked to park in the spot under it and was annoyed that he had to keep cleaning leaves off his car. Never in my life have I felt a desire to key somebody's car—to lay a thick and juicy all-American rip down the side of his Peugeot— but I felt it now. Not that I did anything. Diana was equally angry but more sensible. Once night fell, she simply got a broom and swept the sawdust and leaves off the balcony onto his car below.

Rusk Never Sleeps

I didn't really know what a rusk was until I came to Greece. And when I first picked one up, I was unsure how to eat it without causing serious damage to my teeth. It's an extremely hard piece of brown bread. Like if a stone was made out of barley flour. Throw it at a window and you'll break the glass. It seems inedible, but drench it with fresh olive oil and some chunky tomatoes, letting the bread soften and absorb the liquid—maybe top it with a slice of cheese from Naxos and a grind of black pepper—and a rusk becomes one of those things you eat that is transformational. It is delicious: earthy and nutty and slightly burned. No wonder rusks have been eaten in Athens for thousands of years. Called *paximadia* in Greek, you can find them anywhere. They were in the supermarket, and Artofili, the local bakery, had an entire section of them. The closest thing to a rusk in the United States is melba toast, and that is something every American should be ashamed of. Compared with a rusk, melba toast is embarrassing.

In the ancient world this superhard double-baked bread was valuable because it had shelf life. How could something devoid of moisture go stale or mold? I'm guessing mice, without access to olive oil for dunking, probably wouldn't eat it.

Why do I bring this up? Because *paximadia* was what writers in Athens in the fifth century BCE had for breakfast, although they dipped theirs into a small bowl of wine to soften them. But it's not so different from what writers eat for breakfast today. I typically have toast with guava jelly and café con oat leche.

In many ways, I'm not sure that the life of a writer has changed all that much in the last two thousand years. The technology is different, obviously, because while I'm typing this on an eleven-year-old MacBook Pro, Ariphrades would've sat and scratched out his thoughts and ideas with a metal stylus on a piece of wood covered in wax. A more formal draft would require using a sharpened reed and ink made from ashes and oil on papyrus or parchment. But the essential process was the same: you use language to convey your thoughts and feelings in a way that you find interesting and entertaining. On a good day, your writing surprises you.

Sitting and scratching at wax or clacking on a keyboard isn't the only thing about being a writer. A writer needs to get out in the world, to take the pulse of the street, to immerse themselves in what's happening, to play that old Christopher Isherwood line—"I am a camera"—and observe the humans. This is especially true of comedy writers. To understand what's funny, you actually have to interact with people. And if your style of humor has a political bent, then you'd better keep up on the latest news.

Athenian comedy needed to be as topical as possible when the play went up. Fortunately for writers like Cratinus and Eupolis and Ariphrades, it wasn't a twenty-four-hour news cycle. Maybe more like a twenty-four-month cycle. Things happened a bit slower back then.

With a tip of the hat to English writer Mary Renault, the author of *The Last of the Wine* and other novels set in ancient Athens, let's imagine a day in the life of Ariphrades.

Ariphrades could hear his brother practicing the lyre in the courtyard as he dipped a chunk of barley bread into the terra-cotta bowl and let it soak up some wine. He looked out toward the music and saw Elpis, the slave girl, sweeping leaves into a pile. A few drops of wine squirted into his beard as he bit into the bread and chewed. Despite the wine at the symposium and his late night carousing in the Kerameikos, he'd slept well and felt energetic. Maybe he'd get some work done today.

His father, Automenes, sat down opposite him and rubbed his hands together. His mother carried a bowl of wine and a chunk of bread in from the kitchen and placed it in front of her husband. Automenes nodded in thanks and asked, "Are there any olives?"

She shook her head. "I'll send someone to the market later."

"I can get them. I have to buy some ink."

Automenes smiled. "The writing must be going well."

"I keep crossing things out."

Automenes laughed. "I'm sure the right phrase will come to you."

Ariphrades put the last of his bread into his mouth and wiped his beard with his hand as he chewed. It bothered him when people didn't understand what it took to write, thinking it was easy, as if Thalia whispered words in his ear while he scribbled as fast as he could before the reed dulled. He knew it wasn't because they didn't value his work; they simply had no idea how hard it was, the effort it took to appear effortless. It wasn't simply pratfalls and gags, but real characters conjured to life by his imagination.

He took the back way into the Agora, cutting past the fountain, the Tholos, his bare feet kicking up dust as he skirted the public toilets on his way to the marketplace. He could just begin to hear the clamor of the food sellers when he saw two older men sitting in the shade of a tree near the base of the Temple of Hephaestus. It was Antiphon and Gorgias, renowned teachers and orators, men he knew well as great drinkers of his father's wine and guests often found shuffling around his house looking for a place to piss.

He tried to veer off toward the market, but they intercepted him. Antiphon was the first to wave his hand.

"Ariphrades! Slow down."

The men were twice Ariphrades's age and he didn't want to appear rude. So he stopped and wiped some sweat off his fore-

head with the end of his chiton. "Antiphon. Gorgias. Greetings."
He gave a small bow to the men as they caught up to him.

"What's the rush?" asked Gorgias.

Ariphrades shrugged and watched Gorgias tottering toward
him, a lopsided grin visible through the tangle of his beard.
Antiphon, who was only a few years younger than Gorgias,
gave Ariphrades a strong embrace and said, "How goes the new
play?"

Ariphrades didn't know why, but he didn't like talking
about his work. Not until it was complete. "It is progressing.
But I need to find a good choragus."

Gorgias laughed. "I'm afraid that's as impossible as Persians
making cheese."

Ariphrades didn't know what Gorgias meant by that, but
it was typical of him to spin out metaphors that were unusual,
in-jokes and ironies that only he understood.

Antiphon smiled at Ariphrades and said, "I hope you have
more songs in your play. It's too much ranting these days.
Politics are taking over everything. It's exhausting."

Gorgias disagreed. "Audiences love to watch the shit fly."

Antiphon waggled his finger at Gorgias. "Turd flinging is
not entertainment."

"I'm not sure the prize jury will agree."

"They like it so long as it's not aimed at them," Ariphrades
said. He didn't mean for it to come out so loudly, but discus-
sions of the festival juries sometimes caused his anger to rise.

Antiphon put his arm around Ariphrades and turned him
back toward the shade of the trees. "Explain to these old men
what you are planning. We want to help."

Ariphrades walked with them to the trees and sat on the
ground, letting the shade and a soft breeze cool him off. Gorgias
and Antiphon sat on a bench and looked down at him. The
two men shared a look, as if trying to decide who should speak
first.

Finally Antiphon spoke. "Just because you don't have a tripod doesn't mean you are not respected."

Gorgias nodded in agreement. "I never trust anything with three legs. It's unnatural."

"And don't let Aristophanes's mocking bother you," Antiphon added.

Ariphrades turned to Gorgias. "He mocked you as well. He spares no one."*

"He doesn't like my accent." Gorgias said this in a way that highlighted his light Sicilian accent.

Antiphon chuckled. "Or anything else about you for that matter."

Gorgias laughed. "I am in good company. I would rather be mocked with Cratinus and Ariphrades than be so full of hubris."

Antiphon cocked an eyebrow. "It's hubris he's full of?"

The two men laughed heartily for a moment, and Ariphrades couldn't help himself and chuckled along with them.

Antiphon turned to Ariphrades, suddenly serious. "Listen well, young Ariphrades, the noble families are concerned about some of the conversations they've heard at the assembly."

Ariphrades blinked.

Gorgias tugged on his beard. "They are also full of it. But it is money they're stuffed with."

Antiphon continued. "Some of them don't believe that the people really know what's best for themselves."

Ariphrades laughed. "And they do?"

Gorgias nodded. "The rich always know what's best because they are rich."

"And desire to become richer still," Antiphon said, before adding, "How very wise they are."

---

* In both *Birds* and *Clouds*, Aristophanes mocks the Sophists relentlessly, referring to Gorgias as a barbarian and an opportunist who abuses honest Athenians with his rhetorical skills.

"That's why they fear you, young Ariphrades." Gorgias patted Ariphrades on the shoulder. "You have the ear of the demos."

"I think they fear his tongue," said Antiphon.

Ariphrades smiled good-naturedly. "I bear no grudge against the noble families. I am merely writing about a playwright whose sword has lost its edge."

The two Sophists burst out laughing.

Ariphrades continued: "If someone wants to talk about my sex life, then it is only fair I talk about his. Or the lack thereof."

"I imagine this poor writer is losing his hair." Gorgias chuckled. "With the insults he has hurled over the years, I don't think you'll have a problem finding a choragus after all. In fact, I know someone who will jump at the chance."

Aristotle and Aristophanes have achieved a kind of immortality, but why should Ariphrades all but disappear? Argentinian writer Jorge Luis Borges is quoted as saying, "When writers die they become books, which is, after all, not too bad an incarnation."[1] Ariphrades doesn't get a taste of immortality, he doesn't become a book, because his writings are lost. His incarnation is a small brown Panamanian moth.

The Name of the Moth

There are no physical descriptions of Ariphrades. We don't know what he looked like. There are no busts of him in the British Museum in London or the Getty Villa Museum in Malibu. It's safe to assume he was near the same age as his contemporaries, which would mean he was around twenty-two years old when Aristophanes first called him out in *Knights*.

When I searched for his name online, aside from the mentions in Aristophanes's plays, all I found was a reference to an obscure moth first identified by English entomologist Herbert Druce in his contribution to the *Biologia Centrali-Americana* in 1891.[1]

I find it a bit of a mystery why Druce chose to use Ariphrades as the moniker for this particular insect. Did he lose a bet?

An education in the classics was part of a good education at the time, so we can assume Druce was familiar with the works of Aristophanes, he must've known that the name carried some baggage. Still, can you imagine sailing across the Atlantic; trekking through Central America, battling swarms of malarial mosquitos and amoebic dysentery, hacking your way through the jungle in the heat and humidity, the mud and the afternoon thunderstorms, and climbing up the side of a volcano—basically venturing far outside your comfort zone—and then after all this, all the trials and tribulations, the malaria and cholera and weird tropical fevers, after everything, you discover a heretofore unknown species of insect and name it after an obscure cunnilinguist?

It's not like he took a helicopter to the top of Chiriquí with his butterfly net in his hand. This was old school, late 1880s-style explorer trekking. He could've named the bug after the Queen, or after his parents or a favorite character from history.

And yet, for whatever reason, Herbert Druce dubbed the moth Ariphrades.

It's just weird.

Could it be that Druce named this humble Panamanian moth[2] after a scandalized Greek writer as some kind of in-joke between himself and his fellow lepidopterists? Do lepidopterists go in for that kind of thing? I mean, maybe; Nabokov was a butterfly enthusiast.

Ariphrades, the moth (*from Heterocera no. 40*, Biologia Centrali-Americana, *vol. 4*).

I wanted to know more about how insects are named, so I arranged to meet Brian V. Brown, the curator of entomology at the Natural History Museum of Los Angeles County.

I stood in the central foyer, waiting in the shadow of a massive dinosaur skeleton, when Brian came bounding down the stairs to meet me. He looked younger than you'd expect for someone with his impressive credentials, and he had an easygoing, Hawaiian-shirt-wearing way about him.

"It's a busy day," he declared. "Everybody wants to talk about the painted lady migration."

I wasn't surprised. A billion butterflies were flitting through Los Angeles en masse, something the city that has seen it all had never seen before. The air was so thick with painted ladies that traffic on freeways slowed. It turned out that a combination of unusually heavy rainfall, a super bloom in the desert, and storms near the Mexican border had driven this bumper crop of butterflies off their traditional migration path. It was beautiful. The painted ladies live up to their name: they look a bit like small monarch butterflies, with similar orange-and-black wings. At one point I looked out my window and saw hundreds of thousands of butterflies blowing past my house. It looked like magic.

I followed Brian onto the elevator and we ascended a few floors. He flashed his key card and we got off, into part of the museum where the behind-the-scenes natural history stuff gets done. I wish I could say it was glamorous or high-tech looking, like something Elihas Star* might run crazy experiments in, but mostly it reminded me of an old college office building, complete with wooden doors and frosted-glass windows.

Brian opened a door and stopped to flick on the lights before leading me into a large room filled with ten- or twelve-foot-tall towers of drawers. It turned out to be an insect library. Brian pulled a worn guidebook off a shelf and said, "Let's see if we can find your moth."

He flipped through an index and asked, "Do you know the genus or family name?"[3]

I sighed. The one simple thing I should've brought was the one thing that I had forgotten. "Sorry."

Ariphrades wasn't in the book. Although it turned out to be a book of South American moths and Panama is in Central America, so it wasn't surprising that Druce's moth wasn't there.

We then tried to find the person in charge of the museum's database, but he was out to lunch, and Brian didn't have the password for the database login. If Ariphrades was there, stuck to a pin in a drawer, we wouldn't know.

---

* Aka Egghead, a Marvel Comic character who helped form the Emissaries of Evil.

As a kind of consolation prize, Brian began opening drawers in the stacks. It was astonishing. Hundreds of moths, rows of butterflies of the same species, arranged by the California counties where they were collected. I couldn't tell the difference between a Humboldt County specimen and a Tulare County specimen, they looked exactly the same. I turned to Brian: "Why do they sort them by county?"

He smiled. "The lepidopterists are really into minutiae."

Brian is a specialist in phorids, or very small flies. It's his jam and he gets visibly energized when he talks about the tiny creatures. He showed me some of the flies he'd collected, drawers with hundreds and hundreds of insects so small you can't stick a pin through them, the pin is bigger than the phorid, so they are glued to the side of pins. I needed to take my glasses off and put my face next to the drawer to even see some of them.

"Pretty cool, huh?" He beamed.

I had to admit they were pretty cool.

I followed Brian to a room in the back of the building and we sat around a large wood conference table. He settled into a chair and began to describe the art of naming new species. Unsurprisingly, the first thing you have to do is figure out if you have a new species or not.

"You have to establish some characters that you can use to recognize these things, stable characters that don't vary too much among species. Basically species recognition is by morphology, which you can see, and we look for gaps between individuals. Like one species might be black, one might be red, so that's a morphological gap. These days we're also using DNA a lot for recognizing species, because what looks at first glance like highly variable species is often two or more lineages that are only recognizable retrospectively."

That was step one.

Brian continued, ticking things off with his fingers. "You prepare a scientific paper describing it. You describe all the salient features, list your material, specimens examined; you put it in the context of the rest of the fauna. You write it up and submit it to a journal for publication." He leaned forward and added, "To be officially recognized, a species name has to be published."

Brian made it sound easy, but I suspect it is not that simple. The science has to be on point. Before they can be published, the papers are peer-reviewed, but discovering a new species seems fairly straightforward.

"Are there any rules for deciding on the name?" I asked.

Brian nodded. "The name has to follow certain guidelines from the International Commission on Zoological Nomenclature. You've seen the code?"

I shook my head. "I have not."

He got up from his chair and took a worn green book off a shelf and slid it in front of me. It was titled *International Code of Zoological Nomenclature.* Opening it and glancing at the pages was like staring into a world where everyone spoke backward. I looked up at him, hopeful that he didn't expect me to read it.

"The code gives guidelines for names. For instance I wanted to name a new species I had a couple years ago. It's the world's smallest fly. I called it *Megapropodiphora arnoldi.* I named it after Arnold Schwarzenegger because it has these giant forelegs. I had a great picture of Arnold doing his most muscular pose, the biceps pose, and my fly posed the same way."

He showed me a picture of the tiny fly, and I had to admit that the *Megapropodiphora arnoldi* did look a bit like Schwarzenegger, only cuter.

"There are other ways to derive names, depending on what you want to do. If you want to do descriptive things, like *albitarse*, which is 'white legged' or 'white footed,' that kind of stuff, you have to know a little bit of Latin to get the derivation of your names. But naming things after people is pretty well accepted. Sometimes people buy names, or they give a researcher a donation and out of gratitude the researcher will name a species for somebody. Some people don't like that, they think it upsets the purity of science."

"Does it?" I asked.

"I think that there are so many species that need names, if someone wants to pay me for one of them I'm happy to name one after them."

"So you can pretty much pull a name out of a hat?"

He nodded. "People have named things after *Star Wars* characters, famous actors and actresses. It's kind of desperation. I've described about six hundred species in my career so far and it gets hard after a while, especially within a genus where you've got to have a different name for every species."

It occurred to me that I had been living with the impression that the majority of life on this planet had already been mapped out, collected, and categorized. "Haven't we discovered all the animals and insects already?"

He smiled. "Obviously not. If we're talking about mammals, there's still a dozen or so unknown species discovered every year. Insects, there's thousands discovered every year. I could discover a thousand species every year for the rest of my life and not run out of species to describe."

The only thing holding him back was funding and a shortage of scientists.

"There's not enough experts in the whole world to cover every animal. There are groups that we call 'orphan groups.' Nobody works on them."

The idea that there are orphan groups—living creatures that no one is interested in studying—felt deeply disconcerting to me. Are people so busy looking at their Instagram feeds that they can't muster the enthusiasm to study living creatures? Natural phenomena that exist on this planet? No takers? Really? I would rather look at bacteria growing inside worms that live in a geothermal geyser or study the sex life of a geoduck than watch Instagram "influencers" try to sell me crap or follow the latest nitwit exploits of a YouTuber.

"That's sad," I said.

Brian agreed. "It is sad. When I started working on the flies that I work on there was only one other person working on them really. I had to learn everything from the literature. I never really had a mentor who would teach me this stuff. But there's always somebody who wants to study these little things, you know, there's always interest if you can provide the funding for it. That's the main limitation . . . what is apparently not economically important or directly important to humans. But the thing is we never know when we're going to need basic scientific knowledge. We never know when your moth from Central America is going to provide some scientific information that is desperately needed."

I liked the idea of Ariphrades, the moth, making a name for itself by saving the world from some kind of Chiriquí fever. Because otherwise naming an obscure brown moth from Panama after an even more obscure comic writer from ancient Athens seems completely random.

Brian had to get back to work, the media fascination with the painted lady migration was not going to wait—and how often does the curator of entomology get to hold a press conference?—so we ended the interview. Brian escorted me out of the backstage area, and, as he walked me into the main hall of the museum, he stopped and said, "You know those old entomologists were probably just showing off with the Greek names."

And then he smiled and walked off.

The Antagonist of the Piece

A riphrades can't defend himself in the debate with Aristophanes. His work is gone. So maybe the best way to understand him is to take a look at the man who singled him out for public humiliation: Aristophanes, the big swinging cock of Athenian comedy. There have been several excellent books written about Aristophanes, but for our purposes, here is a kind of capsule biography of Aristophanes to help us get an idea of what Ariphrades was up against.

Like most of the information we have about ancient Athens, it is sketchy at best, with much of Aristophanes's biography conjectured and freestyled by scholars and historians who have scoured his plays for clues of who he was and where he came from.

Aristophanes was, by any measure, a very successful playwright. His career lasted forty-seven years or so, from 427 BCE to around 380 BCE, and he is credited with writing approximately forty plays. As I said earlier, only eleven survived.

Most encyclopedias say something like: "Aristophanes was the greatest of all Greek comic writers, and the only one whose plays survived." Which, I mean, come on, we have no idea who was the greatest, we know the plays of Aristophanes only because, for whatever reason, his are still around. Surviving does not necessarily make you the greatest of all time. Just ask Charles Darwin. However, to his credit, Aristophanes posted some impressive stats. He racked up eight wins and five second-place showings at festivals. By comparison, his nearest competitors over the same period were Cratinus, with one win and three second-place finishes, and Eupolis, four wins and one second place.

You could say that Aristophanes disliked Cratinus as much as he appears to have disliked Ariphrades. Cratinus was older than Aristophanes and apparently had a taste for wine in much the same way Ariphrades had a taste for pussy. Cratinus's big hit was a semiautobiographical play called *Wine Flask*, in which Comedy herself implores a drunk writer to sober up. *Wine Flask* beat Aristophanes's *Clouds* at the Dionysia competition in 423 BCE, which must have been sweet for Cratinus, because just two years earlier, at the Lenaia competition, Aristophanes placed first with *Acharnians*, while Cratinus's *Storm-Tossed* was second. Of course Aristophanes couldn't resist dumping on Cratinus in *Acharnians*, describing an attempted mugging that ends with the character defending himself by hurling what he thinks is a stone, only to nail Cratinus in the face with a fresh turd.

> *When he wants to throw*
> *A stone at him, may he grab instead*
> *Some just-fresh shit in his hand in the dark:*
> *Then run at him*
> *With a rock, and miss,*
> *And hit Cratinus.*[1]

Later, in *Peace*, Aristophanes attributes the death of Cratinus to the Spartan invasion and how he "couldn't survive seeing a pitcher of wine smashed."[2] Of course, Cratinus is quoted as saying, "You will never create anything great by drinking water." Which is a) true, and b) evidence that maybe he did enjoy his wine, and c) maybe a sign I'm reading Aristophanes all wrong and he was simply trying a kind of intervention out of concern for the health of his friend and competitor.

We don't have to read academic studies to get an idea of what Aristophanes was like as a person; we can hear from the artist himself, because much like Muhammad Ali and Eminem,

Aristophanes was not shy about proclaiming his greatness. In almost all his surviving comedies, there are sections called the "parabasis" that have no connection to the plot or anything that has happened or will happen; they're bizarre time-outs where the chorus brags about the playwright's awesomeness and reassures the audience that they are in the hands of the best writer in the world. Sometimes they speak directly to the audience in the voice of the playwright. Aristophanes likes a humblebrag, he doesn't let his brilliance go to his head: "And when he was raised to greatness, and honored as nobody has ever been among you, he says he didn't end up getting above himself, nor did he puff up with pride, nor did he gallivant around the wrestling-schools, making passes."[3] That's right, he's a genius with a street full of tripods, but he's no pedo.

He gets his inspiration from "holding the reins of a team of Muses that were his, not someone else's."[4] You see, Aristophanes doesn't use your common, everyday Muses. Thalia wasn't whispering in his ear. He's got his own muses, because in his world, everything is top shelf.

When he's not bragging, he's dumping on his rivals. In his play *Frogs*, the character of Dionysus goes to Hades on a mission to bring back Euripides because the remaining writers in Athens aren't quite up to the level the dramatic arts demand. Kind of like Bill Murray going into the afterlife to find Lenny Bruce and Sam Kinison because comedy is getting stale. What transpires is a kind of slanging duel between Euripides and Aeschylus in the afterlife, and both of the tragedians are shown to be fusty old hacks. Some of the other playwrights Aristophanes takes down along the way are Eupolis, Phrynichus, and Hermippos. Aristophanes mocks these writers as "boring and crude," whose works cannot compare with "such masterpieces of his own as *Banqueters*."[5]

It is not dissimilar from modern-day rappers who put down their competitors while boasting about their skills, as in

Lil Wayne's classic line "I'm fly as fuck, you ain't even next to depart."[6]

I think we can assume that Cratinus, Eupolis, and the other writers at the time gave as good as they got and insulted Aristophanes as robustly as he insulted them. There are surviving fragments that give us some insight into what the other writers said. For example this excellent fragment from *Toadies*, in which Eupolis comments on someone with a fondness for the good life:

> *Who smells of the fine things in life,*
> *walks with cheeks spread wide,*
> *shits out sesame cakes,*
> *and coughs up apples.*[7]

And as Lucian, our first-century CE satirist, wrote in *Fishermen*: "For so it is with the great public; it loves a master of flouts and jeers, and loves him in proportion to the grandeur of what he assails; you know how it delighted long ago in Aristophanes and Eupolis, when they caricatured our Socrates on the stage and wove farcical comedies around him."[8]

There is no accounting for taste. But still, boasting and slinging insults seem like a weird way to entertain the masses. Horace, another Roman, wrote, "Eupolis, Cratinus, and Aristophanes and indeed any of the other poets of Old Comedy would single out with great freedom anyone who was worthy of being pointed out, for being a wicked man or a thief, an adulterer or a cutthroat or notorious for any other reason."[9]

I like the "notorious for any other reason," because you could become notorious for whatever reason one of these writers decided to make you notorious for when they called you out. You didn't have to do anything.

It was weaponized comedy. Throwing jokes like Bruce Lee threw punches.

Aristophanes saved some of his most savage roasts for a prominent Athenian politician and theater producer named Kleon.

Even though Athens was a democracy, the affairs of the city were by and large run by a group of aristocratic families. Kleon was not an aristocrat. He came from a family of merchants, apparently in the business of the manufacture and sale of leather goods, and found his way into politics. Conservative Athenians didn't appreciate his style. According to Aristotle, "Cleon son of Cleaenetus who is thought to have done the most to corrupt the people by his impetuous outbursts, and was the first person to use bawling and abuse on the platform, and to gird up his cloak before making a public speech, all other persons speaking in orderly fashion."[10] He was, by all accounts, something of a dick-swinging hothead, a warmonger, and a first-class rabble-rouser who once suggested putting down an uprising on Lesbos by killing all the men and selling the wives and children.*

Like a lot of tough-talking politicians, Kleon was thin-skinned and humorless, especially when it came to jokes at his expense. He sued Aristophanes several times, dragging him into court for making jokes about the city and for slander. The verdict must have gone in his favor too: for a while Aristophanes was banned from presenting plays at the Dionysia. Which didn't stop the playwright from continuing to mock and ridicule the politician in subsequent plays at the Lenaia festival.

Kleon challenged the status quo with a street-savvy style that was apparently popular with the poorer citizens of Athens. His popularity—much like the popularity of former reality television hosts who enter the political arena—became a threat

---

* Ultimately cooler heads prevailed, and a compromise was reached where only about a thousand men were executed.

to the aristocracy. That meant Aristophanes. He was the son of wealthy landowners, a member of the aristocracy who had been educated and supported by the aristocracy. In Athens, like everywhere throughout history, aristocrats thought they were smarter than everyone else and deserved to boss things. It's the same tension that animates our politics today, when aristocrats and oligarchs get together at Davos and try to figure out what's best for the billions of people who don't have private jets.

At the time he was growing up, Athens was the center of learning and Aristophanes would've been well versed in philosophy, literature—particularly the works of Homer—and the natural sciences. He would've received the best education available. Pampered, protected, and smarter than everyone else; he seems like one of those kids whose parents tell them they're geniuses when they're really just precocious.

One thing for sure, he was a fan of the old-school way of doing things. In *Clouds* he stages a debate between a character named Mr. Good Reason and a character named Mr. Bad Reason. At one point, Good Reason describes a proper Athenian education: "I'll tell you then the kind of education that once prevailed. When I flourished for holding upright views and self-control was a virtue."[11]

The writer and philosopher Plato backs this up with his description of the Athenian education system in *Protagoras*: "that the child may excel, and as each act and word occurs they teach and impress upon him that this is just, and that unjust, one thing noble, another base, one holy, another unholy, and that he is to do this, and not do that. If he readily obeys,—so; but if not, they treat him as a bent and twisted piece of wood and straighten him with threats and blows."[12]

Yet for a playwright who was happy to make obscene jokes about sex and sodomy, about masturbation and having radishes shoved up your ass, Aristophanes is sometimes really prudish. As Good Reason continues in *Clouds*:

At the trainers[13] a boy had to sit with his
legs crossed so's not to torment any viewer
with lust, and when he stood up he had
to smooth down the sand so's to erase the
imprint of his young virility from the gaze
of any gloaters. In those days no boy would
anoint himself with oil below the navel, and
his genitals were a marvel in their downy,
dewy bloom—like ripe apricots.[14]

Maybe "prudish" isn't the right word. But have you ever
known anyone to be turned on by a dick print in the sand? Or
was Aristophanes worried that he didn't measure up?

It makes me think that, for all his braggadocio, Aristophanes
was shy when it came to sexual matters. It's one thing to make
jokes about it, another to worry that someone is going to stare
at your skid marks. It's reasonable to assume that since his
attacks on Cratinus and his wineaholism were based in fact,
his accusations about Ariphrades were also rooted in reality. I
guess seeing someone gleefully put his tongue in a lady's hot
spot must've gotten his apricots in a twist.

Or it could be that Aristophanes disliked Ariphrades
because his plays were street. Was Ariphrades, like Kleon,
speaking for the common Athenian? The hoi polloi? Why
was Ariphrades the target of so many of Aristophanes's
attacks? What if Ariphrades's plays, like Kleon and others
in the assembly, spoke against the aristocracy? What if his
comedy attacked the patriarchy? Why else would Aristophanes
try to humiliate him for what was then considered transgressive
sexual activity? Maybe it was personal, maybe it was political. I can only speculate. We know from Aristotle's *Poetics*
that Ariphrades mocked the pretentious. This might account
for his lack of wins in the theater competitions: if the judges
were all members of the aristocracy and his work made

them squirm, well, he wasn't going to be taking home any tripods.

And a tripod was no small thing. Literally.

The base of a tripod in a backyard in the Plaka
(*photograph courtesy of the author*).

The ancient Greeks were extremely competitive. They liked contests. I mean, seriously, they invented the Olympic Games. Footraces, chariot races, wrestling, swimming, warfare, drinking, debating—anything that could be turned into a competitive event was. It's not a big leap from the courts of Athens, where cases were more often than not won on the basis of an orator's performance rather than the actual facts, to lawyers of today persuading a jury. This desire to dominate and win, to increase your standing in the community, to avoid the humiliation of submission or subservience, to be the penetrator not the pene-trated, extended to almost every aspect of life.

Much like today's Academy Awards—although much bigger and more impressive than the Oscar statuette—a tripod was the trophy for the winning play at the festivals. Credits were inscribed on the base of the tripod, like a credit roll at the end of a film, and included the choragus as well as the playwright, the musicians, and sometimes the local magistrates. Being a choragus was considered a civic duty by Athenians, and it was an honor for a wealthy citizen to fund a production and give something back to the community. Which is not exactly how producers work nowadays. I'm tempted to make a joke about producers not giving much back to the community except STDs. But I would never do that. That's too easy.

It shows how important theater was to the ancient Athenians that these trophies were sometimes very big, like the Choragic Monument of Lysicrates, which looks to be about thirty feet tall and stands in a little park near the base of the Acropolis.

The Choragic Monument of Lysicrates (*Wikimedia Commons*).

I'd walked past this monument many times, even sat in the park and rested my feet under it, before realizing it was a literary prize. It's a monument that the wealthy patron Lysicrates erected to himself for funding the winning play at the Dionysus festival in 335/334 BCE. It's an impressive piece of gloatery, a magnificent tribute to the ego of the choragus, kind of like Steven Spielberg and George Lucas putting their names on buildings at the University of Southern California. One thing that hasn't changed throughout the course of history: big shots and high rollers still like to remind everyone that they're big shots and high rollers.

Not far from the Choragic Monument of Lysicrates was the Street of Tripods, a path that led from the Temple of Dionysus around to the northeast side of the Acropolis. As you might imagine, the Street of Tripods was lined with various tripods from past festivals. It must have been very impressive. A tribute to the performing arts in the city at the center of the world, the Street of Tripods was kind of like Hollywood Boulevard and the legendary Walk of Fame. But as someone who used to live a few blocks away from this famous part of Los Angeles, I've always thought of Hollywood Boulevard as the "street of disappointed tourists" more than a tribute to the people named in the sidewalk. Although now that I think of it, Aristophanes deserves a star right in front of the Pantages Theatre.

The past couple thousand years have seen a variety of academics trying to make sense of Aristophanes's plays. Naturally there is a tendency among scholars to bend their interpretation of his impact and importance to fit their political and philosophical beliefs. If you were, for example, a nineteenth-century pro-ruling-class monarchist scholar, you might interpret Aristophanes as a raunchy rapscallion who was ultimately an upholder of the ruling class. Likewise, more modern scholars have thought him to be a voice of the Athenian people—a well-educated aristocrat, for sure, but someone who was in touch with what was happening on the streets. Other academics write him off as simply an "entertainer," an unimportant jokester who wrote obscene and offensive comedies to entertain the masses. Philip Walsh, the editor of *Brill's Companion to the Reception of Aristophanes*, writes,

> On the one side is Grote, for whom Aristo-
> phanes is "an indecent parasite pandering
> to the worst inclinations of the Athenian
> rabble"; on the other are Ranke, Bergk and
> Meineke (the German scholars whom Grote
> lists in his history), for whom Aristophanes
> is "a profound philosopher and sober patriot."
> Symonds rejects both views, preferring
> instead "a middle course" when reading the
> plays.[15]

I find all this academic squabbling and freewheeling bias boosting fascinating, but it's also enough to make your head explode, because comedy writing can be both profound *and* indecent, it can pander *and* be sober. A joke can be philosophical and rude simultaneously. That's pretty much what comedy does. That's the pleasure of it. As the first-century BCE historian Dionysius of Halicarnassus wrote in *Art of Rhetoric*, "It is hardly necessary to state that comedy in the time of Cratinus and Aristophanes and Eupolis engaged with politics and philosophy. For in fact comedy is philosophical when it evokes laughter."[16]

Some sources have mentioned that Aristophanes suffered from early-onset male pattern baldness and was acutely embarrassed by this. Most busts portray him with a full head of hair, but this one, I believe, is more accurate:

Not the singer of "Sussudio" (*Illustration by Jaya Nicely*).

Don't misunderstand me, he might look like Phil Collins, but I'm a fan of Aristophanes. I think the way he imagined and invented a theatrical universe is brilliant; his work has everything I like: it's conceptually daring, raunchy, and filled with clever wordplay. And his plays still resonate—the jokes still make me laugh, punch lines landing more than two thousand years after they were written. That says a lot about the power of his writing.

There's not a lot of information about the costumes and masks of the ancient comedies. The props and wardrobe disintegrated long ago. We only know a little about the staging and the set design. Classicists have tried to fill in these gaps by speculating how they think the plays would've been staged, but these are mostly educated guesses. We do know performers wore masks and that some of the costumes were vibrant and outlandish. There are images on ancient pottery depicting men dressed as birds with giant erections dancing around an aulos player, and the speculation is that this represents a "production still" from Aristophanes's *Birds.* But who knows? It could simply be that dressing up like sexually aroused fowl was a fun thing people did.

The comedies typically featured song and dance numbers, and it would be wonderful to see what these might've looked like. Would they be choreographed like a Bob Fosse musical, all sharp and jazzy? Or would they be free-form mayhem, like the Sahara Tent at Coachella? Maybe one of these days I'll get dressed up in a frog costume with a huge phallus and dance through the streets of Los Angeles. Perhaps then—right before my arrest—I'll have an idea of how these ancient performers felt. Otherwise, we just don't know.

I imagine the wardrobe, scenery, and staging of Ariphrades's plays followed the style of the day and he would have used the same basic story structure as well. Perhaps the main difference was that his humor was raunchier, cruder, and more street than that of Cratinus or Aristophanes, tinged with a disdain for the aristocracy, a mocking eye roll toward the habits and beliefs of the ruling class and academia. Maybe, like me, he had a problem with authority figures.

Clouds

There are not a lot of productions of Aristophanes's plays these days. It's more likely that you'd see one of the famous tragedies by Euripides or Aeschylus produced. So when I learned that the Athens & Epidaurus Festival was presenting a production of *Clouds*, directed by the up-and-coming theater visionary Dimitris Karantzas and performed in the ancient Greek amphitheater of Epidaurus, I secured tickets.

The ancient theater of Epidaurus was built sometime during the fourth century BCE and was part of the Sanctuary of Asklepios of Epidaurus, an area that was thought to have healing waters and other health-enhancing qualities. It's about a two-hour drive from central Athens along a new freeway. It's on the Peloponnesian side, so you have to go around the Saronic Gulf in a kind of horseshoe shape. Once you leave the sagging industrial outskirts of Athens and drive through the scruffy hills leading to the Corinth Canal, you enter a rich agricultural area with rolling hills of olive trees and citrus, vineyards and views of the ocean. Closer to the theater, you find yourself in a pine-filled forest, not unlike something you'd see in Central California.

Henry Miller describes an epiphany he had there: "At Epidaurus I felt a stillness so intense that for a fraction of a second I heard the great heart of the world beat and I understood the meaning of pain and sorrow."[1]

It sounds nice, but that kind of stillness is in short supply when a play is on. The roads are clogged with buses, taxis, and cars bringing more than eight thousand people to the theater. And even if all that traffic wasn't there, I doubt I would've heard the heart of the world beating over the raucous buzzing of cicadas blasting from the trees.

We were dropped at the entrance and followed the stream of people heading up toward the theater. They were predominantly Athenians, and even though it was hot and buggy in the humid air, people had made an effort; they were dressed for a night out, even if it took a few hours in a chartered bus to get there.

The outdoor theater is tucked into the curve of the hillside at the base of Mount Kynortio, and you kind of wind your way up to it. When we finally came around a bend in the path and could see the amphitheater, I gasped. It is a jaw-dropping piece of architecture, much bigger and more impressive than I expected. And it's not like I hadn't read that it seats fourteen thousand people or seen the pictures, but in person it really is something.

The entry of the chorus (*courtesy of the Athens & Epidaurus Festival*).

This particular amphitheater is known for its acoustics. As legend has it, you can drop a coin on the marble disk in the center of the stage and hear it clearly in the top rows. I knew that the ancient Greeks took theater seriously, that it was an important art form in their society, and when you see this massive work of architecture in person, it underlines all that. Maybe Henry Miller really did hear the heartbeat of the world in Epidaurus.

Clouds was first produced in 423 BCE. It didn't win the prize that year and was considered something of a flop for Aristophanes. After his setback at the festival, Aristophanes did an extensive revision of the play. Since the original version no longer exists, it's hard to know what, exactly, he changed with his rewrite.

The logline for the play goes something like this: Strepsiades is suffering from panic attacks because he's gone deeply in debt to support his son's horse-racing habit. He gets the idea that if he can learn to talk like Socrates and other philosophers, people who can change up from down and down from up, then he can talk his way out of the debts. So Strepsiades goes to the "Thinkery," a school run by Socrates, to learn the ways of slippery rhetoric. Aristophanes mercilessly mocks the nerds who study there.

The play was a response to the rising use of lawsuits to settle differences in Athens and, with it, the engagement of what we nowadays call lawyers. Athenians litigated everything from murder to adultery, inheritances to paternity, and various business squabbles; in other words, pretty much exactly the same kind of thing we litigate now. And much like the bellicose lawyers strutting in front of a jury today, a trial in ancient Athens was a performance. There were typically five hundred or more jurors hearing the case and, just like at the theater, heckling and shouting at the speakers was common. A wealthy litigant would often hire an orator with a beautiful voice and a quick wit to represent him, to play to the jury much like an actor in the Theater of Dionysus. If the orator was entertaining or clever, he would often win the case despite whatever facts might be presented.

Of course in *Clouds* the plan backfires spectacularly, as Strepsiades is too dumb to really learn anything. So he sends his son to try and he succeeds, learning everything he needs to know from Socrates and returning home from the Thinkery a bloviating asshole. Now he wants nothing to do with his father, whom he considers inferior. In the final scene, angry at being duped by the intellectuals who turned his son against him, Strepsiades sets fire to the Thinkery.

The play is very funny, the jokes from ancient times still pack some sting, and the critique of the legal system—with "Right Logic," a kind of stuffy appeal to all that is wholesome and good, versus "Wrong Logic," everything that is sexy and fun—is as apt today as it was in the fifth century BCE. It makes me wonder how good Cratinus's *Wine Flask* was that it took first place.

We settled into our seats—I was grateful to see the slabs of timeworn and pocked stone were covered by thick foam cushions—and chatted with a few other journalists in the press section.* The sky began to darken and the theater filled. Occasionally there would be bursts of applause from the audience. A few times I thought the chorus was entering and clapped along, but was quickly admonished by a reviewer from an Athens newspaper, a smartly dressed man with blue-framed spectacles, who shook his head sadly and told me that was "something people in the cheap seats did to get the show going." Fortunately the play began before I could make any other faux pas.

Just like this book, classic Greek comedies start with the entrance of the chorus, or *parodos*, as it's called. The light shifted, the crowd hushed, and a troupe of actors dressed as drag queens, plushies, supermodels, and steampunk hipsters

---

* A big thank you to the Athens & Epidaurus Festival for providing me with such good seats!

entered the theater in a straight line, walking in step, arms swinging in unison, their serious expressions at odds with their extravagant costumes. The line moved in a serpentine fashion around the stage, sometimes performing a stutter step or stopping suddenly and swaying backward. It was a kind of sanctification of the comedic space, farcical and yet ritualistic—as if they were giving us a heads-up that something important, sacred, and weird was about to take place. As Stephen Halliwell writes, "Aristophanes always treats it as a theatrical event in its own right: he organizes the parodos, which was clearly a formal convention long before his time, in such a way as to create a specific and usually extravagant effect on the situation in hand."[2]

And then the play began.

The main set was a large cube that represented the Thinkery in the play. It was an ingenious construction; various panels could open or close or be reconfigured into catwalks and platforms. Near the beginning of the play, when Strepsiades approaches the Thinkery, panels opened to reveal a trio of naked buttocks pointed out at the audience. Strepsiades asks one of the Thinkery's students what they are doing. The student exclaimed, "They're trying to see what's underneath hell."

Strepsiades scratched his head. "With bottoms gazing at the heavens?"

"Yes, independently studying the stars."

There's a lot of classic setup–punch line joke structure in Aristophanes's work. And the cast was superb, getting maximum comic effect out of the dialogue and situations without resorting to mugging. When slapstick was called for, it felt natural, and that's not such an easy thing to pull off.

And then the part of the play called the parabasis kicked into gear. Halliwell translates *parabasis* as "stepping forward," the point in the play where the main action stops and the chorus speaks directly to the audience. As discussed in previous

chapters, this is the section where Aristophanes typically un-
loads his list of grievances, boasts relentlessly, and singles out
prominent Athenians for mockery. In this excerpt he berates
the audience for not giving the tripod to *Clouds* when it was
first performed.

> *It was because I believed you sophisticated spectators*
> *And took this comedy to be the cleverest of all my plays*
> *That I deemed it right for you to be the first to savour a work*
> *That caused me so much effort. Yet I left the theatre defeated*
> *By vulgar rivals, an ignominious fate! That's why I blame you,*
> *You "clever" spectators, for all the trouble this caused me.*[3]

I feel for Aristophanes, and I can relate—who hasn't felt
misunderstood and underappreciated? But can you imagine
Martin Scorsese having an actor stop in the middle of his new
film to lambaste the audience because the director didn't win
the Oscar for his last film? No. You cannot. But that is exactly
what Aristophanes is doing.

When you read the parabasis on the page, it feels like a
list of demands, the affect somewhat flat, like a video made
by a kidnapper. But in the unhinged and brilliant parabasis of
Clouds as directed by Karantzas, the chorus—the plushies, drag
queens, supermodels, etcetera—careen and cavort around the
stage at maximum volume, like escaped circus performers,
turning Aristophanes's complaints into a ferocious and highly entertaining rant and rumble. Karantzas had added some
in-jokes for the audience, including a hilarious moment when
one of the chorus removed a coin from her purse and silenced
the crowd so we could hear "the legend of Epidaurus." More
than nine thousand people became weirdly silent, and then she
dropped the coin on the marble disk at the center of the stage.
If the subsequent cheer was anything to go by, you really could
hear it all the way at the top of the theater.

The parabasis was, for me anyway, the highlight of the production.

Karyofyllia Karabeti as Good Reason
(*courtesy of the Athens & Epidaurus Festival*).

The other was when the actress Karyofyllia Karabeti, playing the character Good Reason, ran into the audience and planted a kiss on the top of my head.

The kiss of Good Reason (*selfie courtesy of the author*).

Clouds is dedicated to mocking Socrates, and some historians have suggested that this comedy may have turned the people of Athens against him, leading to his eventual conviction and death. Personally, I doubt it. The timeline doesn't hold up—there were twenty-four years between the performance of *Clouds* in 423 BCE and Socrates's trial in 399 BCE. That said, Socrates's style of questioning every person he encountered and challenging his unexamined beliefs could have become annoying. Imagine going to the grocery store and having a very smart philosopher follow you around, asking you what you thought about the morality of using a plastic bag to hold your avocados, and why do you assume that everything in the store is there for your convenience, and have you actually thought through your motivations for making guacamole in the first place? Socrates taught this method of critical thinking—the questioning of everything—to his students. It sounds exhausting, but it's what we need more of in the world today. A social media disinformation campaign can only be successful if it's accepted at face value and not examined with a critical eye. People in power never like critical thinkers, and no one likes to have to explain themselves, and that's probably all the motivation the city needed to condemn the philosopher.

Aristophanes was clever about choosing the targets for his japes. Socrates was well known in Athens, somewhat controversial, and definitely a person who didn't conform to the standards of the time. In other words, he was an easy target for parody. But that was part of Aristophanes's comedic strategy—if you want your jokes to land, you need to make sure your audience knows whom you're talking about, that they are prominent enough figures to knock off their pedestal. To quote from Halliwell's excellent introduction to his translation of *Clouds*,

> In the case of many "victims" of satire, comic
> prominence should be taken as a reflection

less of scandalous notoriety than of the achievement of status and power within the city. This is most obviously true of leading politicians, generals, and office-holders (Perikles, Kleon, Hyperbolos, Lamachos, etc.), and while our evidence is often inadequate for certainty, we can be confident that this was true of many of the lesser targets as well.[4]

Was Ariphrades as talented as Euripides and Aeschylus? Was he as important an Athenian as Pericles and Kleon? We'll never know. But chances are he was, and if he was, why has history worked so diligently to erase him?

It's not really something I put on my résumé, not something I mention, like, ever, but I have been an actor in an acclaimed, tripod-winning Greek play. This wasn't a nonspeaking part, I didn't just bring a message from the king or stand around holding a spear; I performed the role of Aegisthus in a production of *Agamemnon*—part of a trilogy called the Oresteia written by the famed tragedian Aeschylus. It's a great trilogy, with all the backstabbing and reversals you'd expect from a good telenovela or a *Game of Thrones* spinoff. Written twenty-five years before *Clouds*, the Oresteia won first prize at the Dionysia festival in 458 BCE, so this was a play with pedigree. The version I was in was an experimental adaptation directed by an affable, loose-limbed young man named Mark Anderson and performed at the Odd Fellows Hall in Seattle, Washington. This happened in 1983 CE.

I can't credibly claim that I was acting, since I don't know how to act, and so why I was cast is a bit of a mystery. At the time I was in a locally popular alt rock band called 3 Swimmers, and I suppose Mark might've thought that I was a juicy bit of stunt casting. You know, good for box office. Like putting Madonna in a production of David Mamet's *Speed-the-Plow*.* Mark is now the co–artistic director of Theatre Gigante in Milwaukee and a well-respected monologist. I can only hope he learned from his mistake and never casts a nonacting guitarist in a lead role again. Despite my limited abilities, I'm always up for a challenge, and it was fun to attempt to play Clytemnestra's scheming lover, a louche and debauched man-about-town. Now that I think about it, given my lifestyle at the time, it may have been a clever bit of typecasting.

For those of you not familiar with the story, here's a brief description:

Clytemnestra, King Agamemnon's wife, is pissed because Agamemnon sacrificed their daughter to ensure good sailing when he went off to battle. Aegisthus—that's who I played—is holding a grudge because Agamemnon's father boiled Aegisthus's brothers and served them for dinner. Because of these murders, both Aegisthus and Clytemnestra understandably have a lot of issues and emotional baggage. Their conflicted feelings about Agamemnon bring them together and they embark on a torrid affair, getting it on while they plot revenge. I can't say it's the best foundation for a healthy relationship, but love is strange.

As I said, the production was experimental—influenced by interdisciplinary theater artist Ping Chong—with lots of multimedia bells and whistles. There were drawings by artist Lynda Barry projected on the set, videos filmed on the Puget Sound ferry, and cool sound effects. I know I wore tennis whites and carried a wooden tennis racket instead of a sword. When I asked Mark what he recalled about the production he said,

---

* I actually saw this production on Broadway. Imagine a play where people hold up their lighters at the curtain call.

"One thing I remember clearly was your decision—in some scene, don't remember—to stand in the posture that a wide receiver might stand in at the line of scrimmage—upright, one foot slightly back, leg bent, toe resting on the turf/stage, arms akimbo. Remember?"

I do remember doing that. Why I did it, why Aeschylus somehow inspired me to stand like Otis Taylor, I cannot explain.

Stickin' it to the Man (*Wikimedia Commons*).

One thing I can safely say about the experience: I am a terrible actor.

Although now that I reflect on it, my life in Seattle did have an Aegisthus-like quality. A debauched pretender to the throne involved with a powerful and Machiavellian queen (or two), Aegisthus was riding a one-man rager until Agamemnon's son, Orestes, came to town and dispatched him without hesitation.

My downfall was less dramatic. The band broke up. The relationship(s) fizzled. I got fired from my restaurant job. Everything ended in failure. Although I will say that I became quite good at waiting tables, and that's a transferable skill. But I don't look at any of this as tragic. And, in all fairness, failure is in the eye of the beholder, some people might think I was successful. But I don't mind calling it a failure. Being involved in the arts requires a willingness to fail, to flash and crash and burn. A creative life is full of risks, mistakes, and brushes with stupidity. Hopefully no one dies and you learn some things about yourself and maybe even have fun while you're doing it. But you have to take a step into the unknown and be prepared to fall flat on your face. Samuel Beckett famously said, "Ever tried. Ever failed. No matter. Try again. Fail again. Fail better."[5] Which is the best advice for writers ever given.

I bring up all this to give some kind of context for thinking about Ariphrades.* We know he was a writer and yet there is no record of him winning, or even placing, in the theatrical competitions. Does that make him a failure? I have a hunch he was probably a hit at the box office, which is why Aristotle knew of him ninety years later. You don't see James Patterson or J. K. Rowling winning the Pulitzer Prize or the National Book Award, but their books are going to be around for a while.

It's impossible to make a case for Ariphrades's writing. The last person who might have seen one of his plays has been dead for two thousand years. And yet he lives on in the work of Aristophanes. Although perhaps not in the way Aristophanes originally intended.

---

* And perhaps this book.

The Arc of Comedy Bends

Not many tourists visit the Pnyx. Maybe because they have trouble saying the name. But more likely they're doing what tourists typically do when they come to Athens: going to the Acropolis, maybe taking in the Acropolis Museum and the Agora, and then jumping on a ferry to the islands. They skip the Kerameikos Museum and the Pnyx, my favorite archaeological sites.

The Pnyx is a rocky outcropping on a hilltop about a kilometer from the Acropolis. And, to be honest, there's not a lot to see on the Pnyx hill. There are some trees and some scruffy shrubs, a few benches, and the Pnyx itself. It's not to be confused with the Sphinx or any other majestic ancient structure. When I first walked up to it, I burst out laughing. It was two stone steps leading to a small platform carved out of the rock. No ruins. No columns. Just a stage about three feet high and the size you'd find in an average karaoke bar. A chain, like the kind of thing you see at a movie theater, was strung between a few stanchions and positioned to discourage people from standing on it. But for me that's part of its charm. The Pnyx is humble. It's not trying to blow you away with soaring architecture or amazing design. It's made out of rock, but Machu Picchu it is not. Its power is not in any columns or statues or archaeological remains; this was a place for ideas. The Pnyx is where Athenian democracy was put into practice.

It was incredibly windy at the top of Pnyx hill. The trees were shaking and dust devils erupted from bare patches of dirt, spinning up in the air, forcing me to close my eyes to protect them from grit. I stood on the other side of the chain, looking at the bare stone steps, smaller than a typical American front porch, and I couldn't help be impressed. It may not look like much, but here was where regular people decided they could figure out how to organize their city and live their lives. They didn't need to take orders from anyone, thank you very much.

The Pynx and the Acropolis (*photograph courtesy of the author*).

Nowadays we take the concept—though perhaps not the reality—of representative democracy for granted, but in the fifth and sixth centuries BCE it was a radical idea. Classicists don't agree on who is responsible for this innovation. Some credit Cleisthenes for flipping the script on the ruling aristocrats of the city and devising a way for the various tribes of Athens to share power; others say Solon brought about the fundamental, egalitarian form of democracy. History has a way of crediting innovative individuals with changing the world, but in my experience it's never just one person. Because Cleisthenes could've said, "Hey, I've got this cool idea where we all share power, dispense justice, and run the city together as equals." And the response might have easily been: "That sounds dumb." Or, if my neighbors in Los Angeles are a reliable metric when they discuss, for example, putting in bike lanes: "No way! You can't repaint the streets! Traffic is already too slow! It will ruin our neighborhood!" Thankfully, the citizens of Athens were more adventurous than your average neighborhood council and agreed that it might be a good idea to administer the city that way. More important, they would each actively take part in running the local government and courts. Archaeologists believe that about six thousand citizens— remember these were all men—would gather on the Pnyx hill and discuss and debate various ideas, the speakers standing on the little stone patio, and then decide on laws or whether to go to war or to fix the price at the local brothels, etcetera, in a public vote. I don't want to idealize it too much—it was still a slave-holding patriarchy—but it was democracy undiluted by special interests; there were no smoky backroom deals, no convention wheeling and dealing, no primary rigging. There was transparency in their democracy because most of the people were engaged in it. It's interesting to note that this kind of democracy was performative—people stood up and gave speeches—and interactive, with a response coming from the crowd. It required participation and a give-and-take that was similar to the theater. Perhaps that's why the men who spoke at the Pnyx, like Kleon and Hyperbolus, were so often mocked in the comedies of the time.

Aside from the main framework for representative democracy, two important and related concepts came out of this. The first is called *parrhêsia*—translated as "unbridled tongue"—which gave every citizen the right to say whatever he wanted, to freely express his thoughts and ideas and opinions without fear. As historian Arlene W. Saxonhouse says in her excellent book *Free Speech and Democracy in Ancient Athens*, "It affirmed the rejection of an awestruck reverence for hierarchical ordering of a society and the ancient traditions that supported it."[1]

Socrates famously practiced *parrhêsia*, dispensing a kind of tough love on his fellow Athenians, challenging them relentlessly about their thoughts and feelings and beliefs. He wasn't afraid to question traditions, the status quo, the way things worked. Socrates did not give a fuck. Or as Saxonhouse writes, "Socrates' failure to blush—to care what others think of him, to be ashamed were he to stand openly with his vulnerabilities revealed—lies behind the decision for the Athenians to execute him." That's because he refused to be affected by the bookend to *parrhêsia*, which is *aidôs*. If people are going to say whatever they want, then society will have to figure out some kind of control for that. For the Athenians it was *aidôs*, or what we now call shame. To speak out and cause another individual shame was considered an act of hubris, which was believed to be against the gods and society and all the codes of conduct that keep people from being bigmouthed barbarians. Hubris was a crime. If you insulted someone or degraded his honor, you could be dragged into court and punished. Which put the brakes on too much *parrhêsia*. Kind of like our current libel laws or the unrestrained public shaming that takes place on social media sites like Twitter. You can say what you want, but watch what you say or you could get canceled.

Naturally writers like Cratinus, Aristophanes, and Eupolis were free to say whatever they wanted in their plays—an unbridled tongue was crucial in comedy; the audience expected their plays to push the boundaries of decorum, to ridicule prominent citizens, and to trade in gossip and innuendo. And yet there is evidence that even the most uninhibited tongue sometimes pumped the brakes. Even a writer who spoke as freely as Aristophanes recognized that not all free speech was necessarily the truth. As the desperate debtor Strepsiades says as he tries to convince his dimwitted son to study with Socrates:

> They say that in there are a couple of Reasons,
> the Good—whatever that may be—and the Bad.
>   And one of those, the Bad—so I am told—the Bad
> can plead the Wrong and make it Right.
>   So all you have to do for me
> is learn the Bad Reason
> and I won't have to pay a penny
> of all those debts I owe because of you.[2]

It's not as if much has changed. The tension between free speech and libel, unbridled tongues and political correctness—that particular dynamic continues to animate our conversations today. Tell a lie enough times, put it on heavy rotation on social media, spin it with the side-eye of alternative facts, and quickly the truth becomes blurry, and if you lose sight of the truth, then a society based on rule of law and free expression can begin to wobble. It may have been his personal experience with litigation for insulting Kleon, or it may have been his fear of the populism of the day—the demos wound up by a smooth-talking orator could get you booted out of the city—but Aristophanes was sending a warning to the people of Athens in the best way he knew how: in the form of a joke.

You can see echoes of the Athenian desire for *parrhêsia* if you stroll through Exarchia: the street art and political graffiti that cover virtually every surface of the neighborhood are an extension of that original impulse that turned the Pnyx into the center of democratic Athens. They are the unbridled tongue presented with a can of spray paint.

Yanis Varoufakis Is in the House (of Parliament)

On the other end of the phone, newly elected member of the Greek Parliament Yanis Varoufakis let out a sigh. "This new government . . . they're introducing three new bills that will really do some damage. So I've got to be on the floor of parliament every day trying to stop them."

I understood, he's a very busy guy. I said, "Someone's got to save the world."

Varoufakis laughed. "I don't know about that. I'm just trying to throw obstacles in their way to slow them down."

Varoufakis is the author of several books. One of my favorites, *Adults in the Room: My Battle with the European and American Deep Establishment*, chronicles his brief time as the finance minister of Greece, where he and the left-leaning Syriza government challenged the European Union to try to fight their way out of austerity. French and German banks had over-leveraged themselves in Greece and, when the 2008 financial crisis hit, would've gone bankrupt if the EU, particularly Germany and the International Monetary Fund, hadn't ridden to the rescue. Of course this was done in a sneaky way, where the EU bailed out the banks and stuck the Greek people with the bill. Varoufakis was not shy about pointing out the obvious and refused to play along. He was right, of course, but that didn't make him any friends and didn't save Greece from austerity. But he is a compelling figure on the international scene, an avid motorcyclist with a shaved head and a quick smile, and someone who stands up to the powers that be and speaks with some legit *parrhêsia* unencumbered by any sense of *aidôs*. As finance minister, he had promised his country he would try to end austerity and he wasn't, as Big Daddy Kane put it, half-steppin'.

Not unlike Socrates, he was betrayed. Sometimes one person standing up and speaking truth can change the world, and so the world scrambles to shut them up, humiliate them, and attempt to shame them into silence. Look at what the adults in the room in the United States tried to do to climate activist Greta Thunberg when she came in 2019 to speak to the United Nations. They lost their shit, calling her a "mentally ill child" and commenting on her physical appearance, as if not looking like a teenage sex symbol somehow negated what she had to say. All she was doing was standing up to the capitalist machine, the economic structures that need continuous growth, exploit working people, and suck resources out of the earth like vampire robots—and money and hope out of the Greek people—and saying *enough*. She drew a line. She didn't ask the grown-ups for permission.

Varoufakis's career as finance minister ended in disaster, but *Adults in the Room* is a fantastic read. The *Guardian* called it "one of the greatest political memoirs of all time,"[1] and in 2019 it was turned into a feature film directed by Greek director Costa-Gavras.

In response to his experience with the "deep establishment," Varoufakis and some other like-minded individuals started a movement to renew democracy called DiEM25. It is a pan-European, multiparty political group organizing to resist the current drift of the EU into a kind of bureaucratic corporate oligarchy designed to exploit the weakest members. Much like the early Athenians, the manifesto for DiEM25 calls for simple democratic reforms. They want full transparency in decision-making by the EU and the "urgent redeployment of existing EU institutions in the pursuit of innovative policies that genuinely address the crises of debt, banking, inadequate investment, rising poverty and migration." Those are just the immediate priorities; longer term they are working toward a pluralist, egalitarian, productive, and ecologically sustainable Europe.[*]

Like his Athenian ancestors, Varoufakis is a believer in democracy. I saw him speak when he was in Los Angeles, and when asked why he was working so hard to bring about democratic reforms, he chuckled and said something about it being necessary and that it was "important to have fun with it." When I spoke with him in Athens, I asked if humor was essential to democracy. Comedy needs democracy, but does democracy need comedy?

He replied, "Absolutely. The most progressive, radical, and paradigm-changing ideas were introduced by Aristophanes via the medium of comedy. For example in the *Ecclesiazusae*, where he introduces the notion of a vote for women and, indeed, of a takeover of the assembly by women opposed to patriarchy, war, and inequality. Without comedy, he would never have been allowed to put such radical ideas to the citizenry."

At the time this play was staged, women were distinctly second-class citizens in Athens and were, as Aristophanes portrays in the play, thought to be lazy, adulterous drunks. The play depicts what would happen if women took over the government. What they do is revolutionary: they re-create society so that all wealth and food are shared, people live together in communal housing, and hot young men are required to sexually satisfy women considered old and ugly. In other words, they create a kind of communist utopia where all friends have benefits. If you ask me, this seems like a good thing. I would happily live in a society like the one Aristophanes describes in *Ecclesiazusae*. But I don't think Aristophanes meant it that way. I can imagine these ideas might have been seen by the patri-

---

[*] I highly recommend a visit to their website: https://diem25.org.

archal society as a cautionary tale—*just look what would happen if women were in charge.* No doubt the men of Athens—the benefactors of a patriarchal war machine—got a good guffaw out of Aristophanes's fanciful tale. Much the same way the CEO of a Fortune 500 company might patronize a female executive and her plan to give family leave to employees.

It is unclear which interpretation Aristophanes was trying to promote. Maybe he was just causing trouble, which is undeniably part of his charm. And yet whatever his motivation, many of the points Aristophanes was trying to make, particularly his opposition to war, got embedded in the jokes and, let's call them, *seeds* were planted in the city's consciousness. I imagine that the women watching the production might have had an entirely different takeaway from the men. They might've thought, Yeah, what if we ran things? and then discussed the play and the ideas with other women. Which might have, in turn, created some changes at the household level, which would then have expanded to the neighborhood, the city, and eventually the world.

While many historians believe Athenian women were seen only as homemakers and reproductive units or safety valves for lust, they did manage to overthrow the oligarchy, who had assumed power in a coup in 411 BCE. A group of noble families calling themselves "the Four Hundred" decided it would be better if they ran things and so they took over. It didn't last long. Apparently the women of Athens climbed up on their roofs and pelted the oligarchs with garbage whenever they walked past. This is yet another thing we can learn from ancient Athens. If the women of the world want to climb on their roofs and throw garbage at Jeff Bezos, Mark Zuckerberg, and the CEO of Goldman Sachs, I'll hold the ladder.

Like Varoufakis said, comedy allows us to imagine things that might normally make us uncomfortable. We can talk about subjects that are forbidden and we can bring a different point of view to solving problems. And it's good for you. The Mayo Clinic reports that studies have shown laughter is beneficial for your overall mental and physical health; it stimulates your organs and increases your circulation, releases endorphins, de-stresses, helps people with anxiety and depression, and is good for your immune system. So why is everyone so serious all the time?

If democracy needs a sense of humor, if radical ideas need to be presented in a way that eases them into our consciousness, why are so many people so quick to denounce comedians and squash uncomfortable conversations? I'm not going to deny that there are comedians who are racist or sexist or just plain bad, but our current climate of political correctness, of the rush to cancel someone for what he or she said, lacks nuance and imagination. Some humor is offensive. That is undeniable. But we don't have the legal right to not be offended.

As Australian comedian and writer Hannah Gadsby said in her 2020 one-woman show, *Douglas*: "Now, if in that bit, you find yourself offended by anything I say in the joke section, please just remember they are just jokes. Even if you find yourself surrounded by people who are laughing at something you find objectionable . . . just remember the golden rule of comedy, which is, if you're in a minority, you do not matter. You don't."

This is not a defense of racist or sexist jokes. All I'm saying is that we might benefit from using humor as a jumping-off point or a way in to thinking about and discussing issues and ideas that make us uncomfortable. A joke about rape is obviously offensive, on many levels, but why someone would think that was something to joke about is worth talking about. Comedy doesn't have to offend; a joke can explain why universal health care might be a good idea or why human rights and rule of law need to be respected. Laughing connects us to our fellow humans. Allowing for *parrhêsia* and then having the ability to sustain a dialogue, to look at uncomfortable and unpleasant topics from multiple angles, to think about why something offends, might actually move the consciousness of society forward. Comedy has power. It might save our democracy.

Tilemachos at Sea

Tilemachos Aidinis is a sailor—a captain for hire who pilots charter boats around the Aegean—and proprietor of a company called Greco Sailing. He is a thoughtful man with an easygoing personality and a great laugh. He is strong and roughly handsome, his skin burnished a deep olive brown by the sun, and looks pretty much like how you'd think a Greek sailor might look, only maybe a little more sophisticated because he lives in Athens and keeps his hair up in a kind of samurai man bun. He is an excellent pilot—I have seen him park a forty-two-foot catamaran in a slip that looked too small for a dinghy. And he knows the small islands in the Cyclades. When our friends were desperate to sail to Santorini despite high winds and great distance, he considered their request long enough to say, "Mmmm. No." Getting there with a strong Meltemi at our back might be fast; coming back up into it, impossible. Instead he promised to "show us the real Greece." Which is how we ended up on a small island like Koufonisia.

One of the more remarkable things about Tilemachos is his ability, almost superpower, to enter any taverna, walk right into the kitchen, and demand, "Show me your fish!" I saw him do this a dozen times. No one ever kicked him out. They would nod and immediately open their refrigerators for him, like he was a government-certified fish inspector. Sometimes they would step aside and let him bend down and look at the fish, or they would give him a fish-by-fish description of where it was caught, how long they'd had it, and how they might cook it. I can't imagine anyone doing something like this in a restaurant in Los Angeles.

Tilemachos is well-read and can talk easily about theology, art, politics, ocean currents, climate change, and Greek theater.

He knows a lot about theater because his partner is Dimitra Papadopoulou, a playwright and actress. Dimitra became famous when she wrote and starred in a hit television show in the early '90s called *Oi Aparadektoi* (*The Inadmissible*), which was a comedic look at everyday Athenian life. Since then she has written and/or acted in dozens of plays and television shows. Most recently her play *Mr. and Mrs. Nicolaides Sex Life,* an interactive comedy about a couple and their therapist, ran for three years in Athens. And if you happen to find yourself watching the Greek-language version of *Finding Nemo,* she is the voice of Dory, the animated fish with ADHD.

In other words, she is a successful Athenian comedy writer, a direct descendant of a long line that connects to Aristophanes and Ariphrades.

I wanted to talk to Dimitra about her experiences, so I arranged to have dinner with her and Tilemachos at a restaurant in the Plaka.

The Plaka is the oldest neighborhood in Athens, a mishmash of small streets and stairways piled on top of each other at the base of the Acropolis. It's jammed with bars and tavernas, sometimes three or four stacked on top of one another in an arbitrary way, and filled with a mix of tourists and locals. Diana and I followed Tilemachos and Dimitra down a street, up some stairs, down an alley, up more stairs to even more stairs, into a courtyard of some kind, to a restaurant that was up a spiral staircase, to a roof that seemingly had no electricity and was lit by candles, so you had to kind of shuffle across the surface, bumping into chairs and tables splayed haphazardly over every usable space, until we came to a hard wooden bench. Somewhere directly above us, the Acropolis loomed. Athenians had probably been stumbling into this place for the last thousand years or so.

It was so dark in the restaurant I couldn't tell if that shadow passing by was a waiter, a customer, or a phantom—some ghost in a chiton—and yet somehow a bottle of wine appeared, followed by tasty little pies filled with spinach and cheese, a beetroot salad, a Greek salad, and some more cheese. It had been hot, almost 100 degrees that day, but now the city was cooling down and a soft breeze was wafting along the roof, guttering the candles and causing my skin to prickle with a sensation that was not at all unpleasant.

Dimitra has sharp, intelligent eyes that flash when she gets excited, and her face is lively and expressive, like those of comic actresses Kristen Wiig and Aubrey Plaza. In other words, she seems made for Hollywood. Refreshingly, she has no interest in the American entertainment-industrial complex: "Because I like to speak Greek. It is a beautiful language." And then, as if I didn't quite understand what she meant, she added, "I feel it more."

Her English is a million times better than my Greek, but still Tilemachos needed to jump in from time to time with a translation. She asked what my book was about, and I told her about Ariphrades and how he was accused of inventing cunnilingus. At first she didn't understand. Tilemachos said, "Could you explain?" I tried again, resisting the urge to act it out. Finally Tilemachos understood and broke into a fit of laughter. He then gave a rapid-fire explanation in Greek. Dimitra gave me a quizzical look and said, "This guy invented the blow job for women?"

Diana shrugged and said, "Welcome to my life."

I turned to Dimitra and nodded. "That's what Aristophanes said."

Dimitra laughed. "Aristophanes wouldn't lie."

And I suppose that's it, because there was no reason for Aristophanes to lie about Ariphrades or Cratinus, and there is no existing record of anyone contradicting him. For Dimitra and Tilemachos it seemed perfectly reasonable that a Greek writer invented cunnilingus; the Greeks invented everything.

She leaned forward and said, "Sex is super important, that is for sure. And the connection between sex and satire is very Greek. It goes deep."

I asked what she meant.

"The connection between Aristophanes, long time ago, and today is very close." She put her two index fingers together to demonstrate how close it was. "It's how Greek people relate. It's like *epitheorisi*."

"What?"

"*Epitheorisi*."

Tilemachos chimed in. "Only in Greece is this. There is a lot of songs and music and dancing and speaking."

Dimitra nodded. "Skits. Sketch. Like cabaret maybe. This comes direct from Aristophanes."

Which immediately brought to mind the unhinged energy of the parabasis in Karantzas's production of *Clouds*. It was like cabaret on mushrooms.

Early *epitheorisi* was equally raunchy and wild, a connection to the drunken phallus parade of the Dionysian revels. Nothing was off-limits. Which doesn't surprise me. Sex is an ideal subject for satire: universal, fundamental, and awkward, it drives people to behave in ways they might normally not; it causes individuals to make bad decisions and noble sacrifices, reveals our humanity, our regrets, and our vulnerabilities and desires. The ancient comedy writers understood that sex was the window into our souls. Sex, and the lengths we go to have it, is what makes us human, and what makes us human is what makes something funny.

Like the ancient comedies, *epitheorisi* was political and timely and spoke to the news of the moment. It was humor and performance rooted in a specific place and time and community. Although nowadays, if you look for something close to *epitheorisi*, it is either a variety show like *Ant and Dec's Saturday Night Takeaway* or *America's Got Talent* or a sketch comedy show like *Saturday Night Live*. Maybe it's me, but I find that kind of programming a bit too polished, watered down for public consumption and not as raw as our current political moment requires. Perhaps closer to the original spirit of *epitheorisi* are some of the performances you might find at the Edinburgh Festival Fringe or in improv sketch comedy groups like the Upright Citizens Brigade.

Dimitra adjusted her scarf and gave me a serious look. "But these days it is dead. Instead, all the new persons they do stand-up comedy. An American kind of joke and laugh."

Dimitra is concerned that the Greeks are losing their unique sense of humor, adopting American stand-up, which she says "is very poor." She shook her head sadly and said something in Greek as she reached for the wine. Tilemachos translated. "This has been the last thirty years. Maybe less. Stand-up comedy replaced *epitheorisi*, which was very, very Greek with roots for centuries."

For a time, *epitheorisi* was wildly popular as a public entertainment. As Aliki Bacopoulou-Halls says in "The Theatre System of Greece," "At its inception, *Epitheorisi* was a form supposedly intended to reflect the perpetual flow of things."[1] In other words it was the news of the day put under a spotlight and mocked a bit, like *The Daily Show* but with songs and skits. Or, as Dimitra says, "You have to be very clear with what happens now, this moment."

Eventually, Bacopoulou-Halls writes, "direct or indirect imposition of censorship soon deprived *epitheorisi* of one of its most pungent elements, political satire, reducing the form, ironically, into a kind of theatre of escape, to which, as original Greek revue, it initially had developed as a reaction."

That censorship came from the traditional funwreckers: a conservative government and the Church.

Sketch comedy, variety shows, commedia dell'arte, vaude-ville, cabaret—call it what you want, all these kinds of entertainments have been around for centuries. What made the original *epitheorisi* different was the unfiltered nature of the discourse, particularly around politics and sex. Tilemachos translated for Dimitra: "The spirit of this is from ancient Greece. Everything is political."

Dimitra nodded approvingly. "Society is political."

We started discussing American politics, which Diana had observed we were refreshingly out of touch with while in Athens. Another bottle of wine arrived as well as a cheese pie with a *kadayif* crust, which is like the best shredded wheat I've ever had. Less successful was an asparagus "soufflé," which was really just a very dry frittata.

I found it funny that a fallen soufflé had arrived when we were discussing sketch comedy, because the rising and falling of this delicate egg dish figures prominently in comic sketches throughout history. A soufflé is the comedy equivalent of the truckload of nitroglycerin transported through the jungle in *Wages of Fear*,[2] although a collapsed soufflé is merely funny, maybe slightly embarrassing to the chef, but nobody is blown to bits. Notable soufflé-as-comic-centerpiece bits have appeared in *The Mary Tyler Moore Show*, *The Golden Girls*, *The Brady Bunch*; even *Star Trek: Deep Space Nine* used a soufflé as a gag. In the 1954 film *Sabrina*, Audrey Hepburn's character learns that a soufflé is an accurate indicator of the state of the heart. In the scene, at a Parisian cooking school, Sabrina's soufflé is a disaster. She forgot to turn on the oven. Which then leads one of the other students, a baron of course, to inform her that "a woman happily in love, she burns the soufflé. A woman unhappily in love, she forgets to turn on the oven." Which made me think that the cook at the restaurant might be heartbroken.

There have been all kinds of comedy throughout human history. We enjoy laughter. A happy(ish) ending makes us feel good. Minor humiliations like a fallen soufflé, a good fart joke, watching pretentious know-it-alls fall on their asses, a simple misunderstanding that gets blown out of proportion, hubris, karma, sex, death, and a skewed kind of comeuppance are all things that have been the basis of comedy for as long as people have been laughing. They just get reworked and repackaged and repurposed. Even the raunchy scatological comedy that is common nowadays is just a recycling of the original Greek comedies.

In an interview in the *Guardian*, writer and director Taika Waititi* says it better than I can.

> Comedy has always, for thousands and thousands of years, been a way of connecting audiences and delivering more profound messages by disarming them and opening them up to receive those messages. Comedy is a way more powerful tool than just straight drama, because with drama, people tend to switch off or feel a sense of guilt, or leave feeling depressed . . . Often it doesn't sit with them as much as a comedy does.[3]

It's funny how things go around. Dimitra explained to us that a producer in Athens had hired her to write a new show of *epitheorisi*. "He has already booked a very nice theater in central Athens." The show, which she would also star in, was slated to open in June 2020, which, if you've ever tried to write and produce a play, is like yesterday.

Dimitra sighed. "It is almost impossible, but I will try to write something."

I asked them if the Greek sense of humor helped them through the economic crisis.

---

* *JoJo Rabbit, Thor: Ragnarok*, etcetera.

Tilemachos said, "That's a tough question to answer. Because the crisis did change our mood. The crisis has drained us from humor, has overcome us. Especially in Athens, the temper is very bad. It's not easy when you are losing your job or your house. On the other hand, the past few years people started to go to the theater again, mostly to see comedies. Laughter liberates you and gives you courage and, most important, unites people."

Dimitra added, "Greeks are ready to laugh with everything."

Decorative Pottery

Deep Ellum is a lively, slightly divey section of downtown Dallas. There are lots of bars and restaurants, a smattering of art galleries, and an excellent independent bookstore named Deep Vellum. I was there to drink some cold beer in a dark bar and see the Austin-based feminist punk band Sailor Poon.[1] With songs like "White Male Meltdown," "Butt Gush," and "The Dick," it feels like Sailor Poon has a spiritual affinity to the raunchy political humor of the early Athenians. I imagine Ariphrades wouldn't be able to resist a band of sex-positive women who proudly proclaim their motto is "Always Crude, Never Prude."

Onstage they have a loose, garage-tinged sound, and like all good punk it's chaotic and fun. The chorus of their song "Leather Daddy" is especially catchy with its demand for oral sex, new shoes, an orgasm, and then a polite request to be left alone. They have manners and an aggressive pro-cunnilingus stance.[*] This attitude would definitely have not been well received in ancient Greece or, I suppose, certain parts of the contemporary American South.

Why do I mention this feminist punk band? Because depictions and mentions of cunnilingus are still relatively rare in Western culture.

UC Berkeley professor of classics Leslie Kurke, in her book *Coins, Bodies, Games, and Gold: The Politics of Meaning in Archaic Greece*, writes about Greek art and the images presented on the coins and pottery of ancient Athens. The book is a coin collector's wet dream, but I'm more interested in the images on the

---

* Also check out Underhairz, a female trip-hop trio from Osaka, and their song "CunnilinguSmile."

decorative pottery. Here she describes a very lively orgy depicted on a cup from circa 510 BCE: a woman is leading a man by his erection, someone is masturbating, a couple is fucking, and

perhaps most remarkably, the woman next to this couple raises her left leg high in dance while a young man reclining in front of her seems to be about to initiate cunnilingus. If this is indeed what the vase depicts (and there is some dispute on the matter), it is the only representation of cunnilingus in all of Greek art. For the protocols of Greek culture regarded oral sex as particularly demeaning for the partner who gave it, so that, while scenes of women fellating men are fairly common, depictions of cunnilingus are almost nonexistent.[2]

Cool trick, bro (*British Museum, Wikimedia Commons*).

Of course, just because an action is depicted on a piece of pottery doesn't mean it's based on fact or an accurate representation of an orgy. Ancient pottery is not a photograph or a selfie. It could be that the artist intended for the pottery to be outrageous and shocking, or perhaps it's exaggerated to be funny, like something R. Crumb might draw if he were in the business of putting his art on ceramics. As classicist Holt N. Parker writes in "Vaseworld: Depiction and Description of Sex in Athens":

> That is, the decorations on pots are too
> often taken as both representations (as if
> the unmediated depiction of practices) and
> representative (as if offering an accurate
> cross-sample of what people actually did).
> This "snapshots of Athenian life" approach
> tends to ignore the facts that even our
> snapshots are controlled, selected, cropped,
> manipulated, intended to convey one picture
> of reality and not another.[3]

I think that they might've been tchotchkes, raunchy pottery for sale to tourists. Sex sells, as they say, and there was a robust trade in Athenian pottery all around the eastern Mediterranean, with titillating vases and erotic wine kraters found in Sicily and parts of southern Italy. You can see the T-shirt, can't you? I TRAVELED ALL THE WAY TO ATHENS AND ALL I GOT WAS A PIECE OF RISQUÉ CROCKERY. Which might mean that—like those tapestries that people always seem to bring back from Peru that depict llamas fucking—there was some exaggeration for commercial effect.

But it seems strange that there are no depictions of cunnilingus. They showed everything else. A quick survey of the erotic pottery of the Athenian ceramicists reveals that, like the comedies, not a lot was considered off-limits. There are numerous depictions of sex: men engaged with sex workers in brothels; flute girls at symposia; people engaged in rear entry, fellatio; women leading men around by their erections; a woman hoisted into the air as someone fucks her and another figure holds what looks like a cup under her butt; and in one notable ceramic, a woman engaging three men at once. There are depictions of men having sex with boys, Greek men sodomizing Persian men, Minotaurs raping villagers, and Satyrs doing whatever the fuck they please. My favorite image is a Satyr balancing a large goblet on the tip of his erect penis while a friend fills his cup.* Satyrs are mythical nature spirits embodying male energy; they sport permanent erections and are typically depicted drunkenly frolicking and doing tricks with their dicks.

OG party rockers, Satyrs will do most anything, but you won't find them using their tongues to pleasure a woman. The absence of images of cunnilingus gives us a clue as to how transgressive it really must have been and how shocking for Ariphrades to become known for doing it.

What we know about ancient Athens, what we glean from these snapshots, is incomplete. It's all shards and fragments—not just the pottery, but scholars and historians use fragments of ancient plays and the existent comedies of Aristophanes to create another kind of snapshot of Athenian life. Combined with the images on the pottery, these provide historians with just enough information to be dangerous to themselves, susceptible to a variety of theories and hypotheses that arise around what it was like to live in that world. One school of thought, proposed by French philosopher Michel Foucault, looks at the power dynamic in sexual relations, with penetration and aggression seen as a positive—the winner!—and being sub-

---

* And people brag about being good at beer pong . . .

missive or penetrated during sex as a negative—the loser!—as a defining characteristic of ancient Athenian relations. For sure there were some power and gender dynamics at play; sex can be a complex web of interconnected social, political, and economic exchanges, or it can be a simple cash transaction. In the competitive culture of Athenian patriarchy, dominating your sexual partner might provide some social uplift; you could, I suppose, earn some props for delivering a proper pounding. But I find that kind of analysis detached from lived experience. For one, the submissive partner might be enjoying him- or herself. Maybe that's just what he or she is into. And if you're into it, isn't it possible to be submissive and still in control of the power dynamic? Because inside the dynamic, power is in the head of the beholder.

In our current political culture, with leaders who grab and grope women, with business CEOs and celebrities who abuse their power and influence for sexual favors, isn't it time for women to take a cue for Karl Marx and seize the means of production? It feels long overdue. Maybe that's what the #metoo movement can accomplish. That's what feminist punk rockers like Sailor Poon do. They take ownership of their sexuality. Of course in ancient times the trope of a sexually aggressive woman was used for jokes or to create horror and revulsion in plays and poetry. I wish I could say things have changed.

It could be that Ariphrades found enjoyment in pleasuring women and that flipped the penetrator-as-winner power dynamic on its head. It showed that you didn't have to dominate to experience pleasure. It questioned the foundation of the patriarchy. What if the obsession with penetration was a sign of insecurity, a flaw, a weakness? The Greeks were obsessed with impotence. As Philodemus writes in a poem to Aphrodite:

> *I, who in earlier times could manage between five*
> *and nine in a session, now, Aphrodite, can scarcely*

achieve one from dusk till dawn.
And, unfortunately, the "thing" itself has, of late,
been more often than not semi-lifeless, and right now
is on the verge of "death." This is the Termerion.
Old age, old age, what do you have to offer later on,
if you do come, when even now I am wasted away?[4]

The reference to Termerion is a funny pun. It refers to a bandit named Termerus who would kill his victims by smashing their head in with his head. Get it? Your head—the tip of your penis—goes soft and you die. Which seems appropriate given the author's lament. What is the use of living if you can't get it up? What is the purpose of life if you can't dominate? Would you then become submissive? Isn't it better to die? You can see where this is going. This is what they're afraid of. Take their erection away and they become crybabies. Remove their ability to dominate and what are you left with? Equality?

Don't Hate the Player, Hate the Game

The concept is simple. A writer sits down with a producer or studio executive and tells a story. This is called a "pitch." If the producer or studio executive likes the pitch, then a sequence of events unfolds that hopefully leads to the writer getting some money to go write the script. If it goes really well, then the producer or studio executive takes the script to a director, who then casts it with actors and a movie or television show is produced. It seems pretty straightforward, and yet 99 percent of the time a pitch is a futile endeavor; the writer tells her story and the producer or studio executive says thanks for coming in. The writer might have worked for months honing the pitch, rehearsing her delivery, making the story as airtight as possible. And then that's it. There's nothing to show for all that work. Although they typically give the writer a bottle of mineral water and validate her parking.

It is a very weird way to make a living, spending sixty minutes in front of a roomful of executives, doing the old dog and pony show, shucking and jiving, hoping you interest them enough for them to put down their smartphones. It's a system that forces introverts and nerds—writers—to become extroverts, to perform, to enthrall the room with a little razzle-dazzle. It's not enough to say, "It's called *Teenage Bounty Hunters* and it's about twin sisters who become bounty hunters."* You have to wow them. How pitches are received changes from executive to executive. Some want a detailed three-act structure with every little beat of the story accounted for; others start checking their text messages as soon as you say, "Act two starts with . . ." It's a crapshoot, a mild indignity writers are put through because

---

* I would green-light that in a heartbeat.

our job requires us to do the work and then get paid. Which I guess is like a baker or a furniture maker or any other artist. But the baker doesn't have to pitch, she just lets the aroma of a freshly baked croissant do the talking.

The Athenian playwrights were no different from Hollywood hucksters in this regard, although the Athenians didn't wear sneakers, jeans, and an old Danzig T-shirt under their Rag & Bone blazer.

Let's go back in time—do the special F/X where the text begins spinning and lap dissolve to 420 BCE—and check out Ariphrades on his way to pitch his play.

Ariphrades walked through the Plaka, winding down narrow streets, past houses tightly stacked along the slope, buildings that looked impressive from the outside but were warrens of cramped spaces inside. He felt beads of sweat forming on his forehead and wiped his brow with the back of his hand. It wasn't hot. He was nervous, on his way to pitch his new play to someone Gorgias had recommended, a wealthy wine importer who he hoped would provide the funding he needed to put on a show that might, once and for all, win a prize. At the very least he hoped it might shut Aristophanes up.

He saw a young woman leaving a house. She didn't look like a slave but was definitely not one of the citizens who lived in the area; what he did notice was the way her chiton clung to her hips. He turned to watch her and almost collided with a muscular young man hurrying down the hill. It was his friend Kosmas.

"Kosmas! Off to the palaestra?"

Kosmas smiled and gave Ariphrades an embrace. "We were just talking about you."

"Something good, I hope?"

Kosmas looked down at the ground.

Ariphrades sighed. "Or not?"

Kosmas shook his head. "I'm being punished."

"Why?"

"Last night I was reading your play, which I was very much enjoying. Too much, it seems. I woke up the house with my laughter."

Ariphrades did a mock bow. "The poet thanks you." Ariphrades saw his friend's expression change.

"My father was pissed. He read some of it and thought it was nasty. He took the scroll away."

"What?"

"He said I shouldn't be wasting my time reading trash."

"I'm sorry."

"You should be. You are too funny."

Ariphrades nodded. "Should I get my scroll from him and apologize?"

Kosmas laughed. "I'll see that it's returned. But you might want to rein it in!"

Ariphrades smiled and spread his hands out with a shrug. "I will endeavor to bore the shit out of everyone with my next play."

Kosmas laughed and started off down the street. "Good man! It will give my father something to talk about."

Ariphrades turned and continued up the hill. He tried not to feel resentful. He came from a family of performers—his brothers were lyre players and actors—and many times the conversation at family meals revolved around the fact that artists and performers had to rely on the wealthy to bankroll their shows. He remembered his brother, Arignotus, drunkenly lamenting a meddlesome patron who had demanded the musicians change a song. His brother had slammed his cup down, cracking the base, and shouted, "I will only play what I want to hear!"

Presenting the idea for his play and asking for patronage left Ariphrades feeling slightly humiliated, like a beggar. It didn't help that two of his usual patrons had decided they couldn't afford to back his chorus this year. The Peace of Nicias had ended the war, and they were more interested in investing in land and trade outside Attica. At least until the next war broke out.

Ariphrades arrived at the house of Leogoras. It was an opulent structure. One befitting a man of wealth, the descendant of a noble family whose son, Andocides, was now one of the most famous orators in Athens. There were statues in front of the house and a small pomegranate tree. Ariphrades stopped for a second and sighed. He and Leogoras had one thing in common: Aristophanes had ruthlessly mocked Leogoras in his play *Wasps*. Ariphrades hoped that the nobleman might have an appetite for revenge.

The old man was sitting on a bench in the courtyard when a slave escorted Ariphrades in. Leogoras smiled. "Here he is! The man with a reputation for eating delicacies as notorious as mine!"

Ariphrades couldn't help but laugh. He felt instantly at ease in Leogoras's presence. "Thank you for seeing me."

Leogoras nodded and smiled. "I should be thanking you. I am an admirer of your plays, and I look forward to watching you shove a radish up Aristophanes's ass."

"That would give me great pleasure."

Leogoras rubbed his hands together and motioned for Ariphrades to sit next to him. "So tell me, how will we fuck him?"

Ariphrades sat and a slave poured them both a cup of wine. He took a sip and began talking. "It's the story of a poet, one who is so arrogant he snubs Calliope, Erato, and Thalia."

"Polyhymnia?"

"All the Muses. He declares himself so brilliant that he has no need for them."

"Sounds like trouble."

"They curse him, turning him impotent."

Leogoras laughed. "I like it."

Ariphrades continued: "Here's where it gets weird. The freshly impotent poet appeals to Priapus for help." Ariphrades paused. "And here I imagine will be the first song and dance. The chorus dressed as donkeys and giant phalli."

Leogoras clapped his hands together in delight. "Yes!"

"Priapus agrees to lift the curse and promises the poet he will never have to worry about an erection again."

"How?"

"By turning him into a woman."

Leogoras slapped his knee. "Much worse than being impotent!"

Ariphrades nodded again. "When he goes to his friends for help, they all try to fuck him. I'm working on the song for that now called 'The Flute Girl Who Wouldn't Blow.'"

"Does he live the rest of his days as a woman?"

"No. He has to lift the spell and turn back into a man."

"How?"

"According to Priapus, he must lick every flute girl in Athens."

Leogoras raised his cup to Ariphrades. "And so his quest begins!"

Ariphrades grinned. "I'm still working out the brothel scenes."

Leogoras patted Ariphrades on the thigh and took a sip of wine. He looked at Ariphrades with a serious expression. "They will hate it, you know."

"I know."

Leogoras smiled. "Then let's make it the best play they've ever hated."

In my experience it's never this easy. The writer might really deliver in the room, the producers and studio executives might be laughing and applauding, they might really "see the movie," but once the writer leaves the room, the producers and executives put their heads together and try to come up with a reason to say no.

Of course sometimes they say yes. I once pitched a novel adaptation to Danny DeVito and his production company. As I was telling the story, DeVito kept rubbing his hands together, laughing and chuckling. Making Danny DeVito laugh is really all the encouragement a person needs. Ever. To do anything. When I was finished DeVito said, "Thank you. This is great."

And we made a deal.

But that's really the exception. A more typical experience is when I pitched what's called a "take"—the writer's idea of how to revise an existing script—to Teddy Zee, an executive at Columbia Pictures, and Moshe Diamant, a well-established producer of mediocre action movies like *Universal Soldier: Day of Reckoning*, *Simon Sez*, and *Dragon Eyes*. I'll be honest with you, I'm not proud that I was spending my time concocting plots for Jean-Claude Van Damme vehicles, but a writer's gotta eat. Besides, my idea about a scallop diver who becomes a reluctant hero was pretty quirky, like if a sous chef was also a highly trained assassin. And it was set in the French Riviera. So there's that.

As I presented my story, Teddy listened and nodded while Moshe chatted with someone on his mobile phone. Occasionally Moshe would speak loudly into the phone and Teddy would mouth, "Just keep going," and make that rolling motion with his fingers. When my spiel was over, Moshe hung up the phone and looked at me. He was silent for a moment, then said, "What about plutonium?"

"He's a scallop diver," I said. I was trying to hide my irritation, but in retrospect I think I probably said it like someone talking to a puppy that just shat on the floor.

Moshe turned to Teddy, then back to me. He was baffled. "Scallops?"

He did not see the action movie potential in harvesting delicious shellfish and I did not get that job. Which is probably just as well.

None of my Hollywood anecdotes—and trust me, I've got loads more—are particularly unusual; putting on a dog and pony show has been the burden of writers since writers started writing. Aristophanes had to do it. So did Aeschylus and Euripides and all the other great writers of the classic stage. They would have to pitch their proposed show to a rich dude, who, if he liked it, would then hire the chorus, pay the actors, and generally fund the production. And if the show won a prize, they put his name in big letters on the tripod. That's how it worked in Athens in the fifth century BCE and that's how it works in Hollywood in the twenty-first century. I'd like to rant against the way capital influences the arts and to demand writers and artists seize the means of production and control their destiny, but except for a few people, I'm not sure it will ever happen. Not in a world where you need millions of dollars for marketing and what they call "P&A" (prints and advertising)—basically the money spent to get your production noticed. At least with books and plays the writer retains the copyright. That doesn't happen in movies and television. Which seems wrong to me. Shouldn't the content creator own the content? But that's not how it works. Because the people with power—the corporate CEOs, the royal families and religious leaders, the presidents and prime ministers, and the military-industrial complex—know that power comes from controlling the story. That's how our brains work. We define the world by creating narratives. Simple stories we learn from childhood to keep us alive: sharks are dangerous, fire can burn, oysters are edible but not always. As we get older we start to notice more and more gaps, the things we don't understand, the unknown unknowns, and our narratives become more complex. Myths remind us of human fallibility and hubris, fairy tales teach us lessons about a world filled with dangers. And when we're confronted with the ultimate mystery—what happens when we die—our narrative brains fill in the gaps with our imagination. This is how religions are born. God is a fiction designed to give us answers to the things we will never know. Some people find that comforting and that's okay, but let's be clear that it is a story. Someone made it up and wrote it down.

Controlling the story is how people in power stay in power. The president of the United States tells us that there is an imminent threat to our interests, and the next thing you know missiles are launched, bombs are dropped, and thousands of men, women, and children die. The truth, the real story, isn't revealed until years later when we learn it was all based on lies and disinformation to increase the value of corporations on Wall Street. And even then no one is held accountable. Which is why an informed populace, who can think critically and see through false narratives, is a threat to the power structure. With corporate media as invested in making profits as they are in finding truth, and social media awash in bizarre and increasingly ludicrous disinformation campaigns, we find ourselves living in a world where it's hard to tell what the narrative is, much less control it. Ariphrades's story is a small example of this. His narrative was destroyed. His life story was reframed as one of debauchery and transgression. My hope in writing this book is to give him some of his story back.

But our need for stories and our telling of stories aren't necessarily a bad thing. They give us life lessons and teach us how to navigate the world. And much of it happens on a completely subconscious level when we're children.

Athos Danellis is one of the last Karagiozis puppeteers in Greece. It's a kind of shadow theater that was once extremely popular in both Turkey and Greece. Light is rear-projected onto a screen, and the two-dimensional puppets perform in silhouette. The rear projection gives the show a dreamlike quality, making the puppets come alive in your imagination in vivid and slightly weird ways that are more David Lynch than Punch and Judy. Perhaps that's the power of the shadow.

Karagiozis is the main character in these stories, a down-on-his-luck trickster who is always scheming to get money and food for himself and his family. Even though he is poor, he is intelligent, mischievous, and a bit of a con man. The trickster is an archetypal character, and you can find one in most folklore, whether it's Loki in Norse mythology, the coyote in Native American stories, or the *kitsune* in Japan. He is in many ways emblematic of the Greek people surviving the financial crisis—they are living by their wits.

Danellis is the founder of the Athens Shadow Theater Company and the Greek Shadow Theater Archives. He also teaches in the theater department at the National and Kapodistrian University of Athens. His specialty is to perform obscure plays from the Karagiozis repertoire.

If you've made it this far into the book, you know that I am a narrative nerd, a sucker for anything to do with stories, books, and libraries—so when I saw that Danellis was performing an obscure play called *The Birth of Kollitiri* at the National Library of Greece, I couldn't resist.

The library is part of the Stavros Niarchos Foundation Cultural Center (SNFCC) in the Kallithea neighborhood of Athens, a once slightly industrial area not far from the busy port of Piraeus. The complex includes the Greek National Opera, a very long man-made lake, and one of the most beautiful parks I have ever seen. The center was designed by Italian architect Renzo Piano, the same architect responsible for the Whitney Museum in New York City, the Centre Pompidou in Paris, the Nasher Sculpture Center in Dallas, and the Academy of Motion Pictures Museum in Los Angeles. He's won the Pritzker

Prize—a very big deal for architects—and a bunch of other fancy awards. In short, he's a total pro. And the SNFCC might be his masterpiece.

The center sits on a hill overlooking the ocean. From the top—what's called the Lighthouse but looks like a spaceship—you get a 360-degree vista from the bay to the Acropolis and the surrounding city. The gardens have been designed with walking paths, fragrant plantings, and a large grassy area where, on my visit, kids were playing soccer and a yoga class was in progress. The entire park is slanted slightly, which is not that great for soccer players, but it means that wherever you are, you get a magnificent view.

The shadow puppet show was being presented on the roof of the opera house, on what's called the Panoramic Steps, which is basically an outdoor amphitheater. The opera house is covered by a massive and audacious canopy contraption that gives the structure its spacecraft look.

(Photograph courtesy of the author)

I got a glass of white wine and stood off to the side, watching a steady flow of parents and small children coming to the steps and sitting in front of the shadow puppet stage. It was not a large screen or anything remotely high-tech looking. The stage looked as if it had once been part of some steampunk circus a hundred years ago. Which is not to say that it was without charm.

The crowd continued to grow—there must've been about a hundred people there—and once the sun dipped below the horizon, the show began. It seems counterintuitive, but you need it to be dark to cast a shadow.

As a voice boomed over the sound system, a small shadow puppet appeared on the screen. Unlike the all-black shadow puppets of Java and Bali, these puppets were drawn so you could see their faces and what they were wearing. Karagiozis was dressed in what I can only call puppety clothes: clunky shoes, knickers, and some kind of old-fashioned tunic. Many of the people he encounters on his journey wear a fez. You don't see many people wearing a fez in Los Angeles, but seeing it on the puppets reminded me of my grandfather, who was a member of the Abdallah Shriners of Kansas City and often wore a rhinestone-bedazzled fez while enthusiastically drinking Jack Daniel's, playing a banjo ukulele, and singing goofy songs. From my experience, if you wear a fez, you're looking for a good time.

I wish I could say that I was as engrossed as the children watching the escapades of Karagiozis. I wish I could say that I laughed along with them. But it was in Greek.

After a while I walked around behind the stage and, despite the security people telling me to move along, watched Danellis and his assistant flip the puppets around, manipulating the sticks to make them dance and express themselves. All the while he kept the story going, jumping in and out of various voices like Mel Blanc doing Bugs Bunny, Foghorn Leghorn, and Pepe Le Pew without missing a beat.

Karagiozis is an old form of theater, from the sixteenth century, and it's weird to see what are basically paper dolls hopping around in the shadows. It is definitely not a Disney movie, and yet the story resonated, the kids were digging it, you could see it on their faces. And even though I had no idea what was happening in the story, I was moved by the endeavor of one of the last Karagiozis puppeteers in Athens; there was something beautiful about watching old-school storytelling connect with modern children, the power of story cutting through the noise of our plugged-in tech-scrolling attention spans.

Ariphrades's head was spinning as he left Leogoras. Not only had the wealthy benefactor guaranteed to fund his chorus, but he was going to hire the best actors and singers available. He wasn't sure if Leogoras was being so generous to annoy Aristophanes, to grab the best performers before he could get them, but then he didn't care. Now he could create elaborate effects like Aristophanes and have beautiful costumes like Eupolis; he could afford singers who would make Cratinus's and Leucon's heads explode. It was a budget beyond his expectations, and it would give him a good chance in the competition.

But with Leogoras's generosity came a newfound sense of anxiety. Ariphrades suddenly felt the burden of expectation, something that he'd managed to avoid in the past when he'd been the upstart, the man of the streets, the underdog snapping at the heels of the more established playwrights. He knew the concept for his play was clever, but now he needed to write it well. Better than well. He needed his words to move the world. More important, he needed a drink.

Ariphrades turned down an alley and into the open patio of a taverna. Night had fallen, the rosy dusk fading to indigo, and the slaves had put out small oil lamps. Ariphrades nodded at a few men sitting together and found a table by himself. An oenochoe of wine and a squat cup were placed in front of him, and, remembering not to drink too much when he was hungry, he ordered some cheese with barley rusks. He poured himself a glass and toasted his luck. Although maybe it wasn't luck. What if he had earned Leogoras's patronage with the brilliance of his idea? His throat was dry and dusty and the wine caught in it and made him cough. Now was not the time to get a big head, now was the time to write like he'd never written before. To really push the boundaries. He coughed again and washed the dust down with a large swallow of wine.

And then he heard a familiar voice. "It would seem your throat is only accustomed to the most feminine of juices. The wine too strong?"

Ariphrades turned to see Aristophanes sitting at a nearby table with Pausanias and Agathon.

"My throat is dry from talking, not licking." Ariphrades looked at Aristophanes and raised an eyebrow. "Aren't you being sued again?"

Aristophanes grunted. "No one can take a joke anymore."

Agathon poured wine for Pausanias and Aristophanes and said, "Except Ariphrades. He does take your barbs with a smile."

Aristophanes nodded. But before he could speak, Ariphrades shrugged and said, "I'm not ashamed."

"There is a difference between being unashamed and shameless," Aristophanes said.

Ariphrades laughed. "I see you've been spending time with Socrates."

Aristophanes shook his head. "He's still angry with me. He also couldn't take a joke and now he's touched by madness."

Pausanias laughed. "At least he didn't take you to court."

"True."

Ariphrades nodded. "When the people stop laughing, only then are we truly fucked."

Aristophanes smiled and lifted his cup. "I pray it never happens."

The men drank from their cups, and then Aristophanes couldn't resist. "I guess we won't be seeing a play from you at the next festival."

"You will."

Aristophanes cocked his head. "You have a sponsor?"

Ariphrades nodded. "Leogoras has been very generous."

Ariphrades watched as the news settled over the next table. Aristophanes looked at Agathon, who smiled wryly, then turned to Ariphrades. "This is going to be fun."

Building Zeta

A short walk from Amazonon Street is the Kerameikos Archaeological Museum. It's on the site of the original Kerameikos, just inside the ancient city gates, and gets its name from the ceramic workshops and studios that used to fill this area. Not only was this a hub of industry, but at night, it was the site of one of the most famous brothels in the city. You can stand in the ruins of this ancient bordello. Some of the walls are still intact, as is the alley that runs between the city wall and the building. You can lean on them, just like flute girls and comedic playwrights might have done 2,500 years ago.

Not surprisingly, the brothels of ancient Athens had menus. I'm guessing the brothels of contemporary Athens probably have menus too. It's always good to know what the various services on offer are and how much they cost. For example in Athens around 420 BCE you could get the *kubda*, which was the cheapest position and involved standing behind the enslaved prostitute, who was bent forward; for a few obols more you could spring for the *lordō*, which was the same as the *kubda* but with the enslaved woman leaning back against you, or you could go all out and try the *keles*, or "stallion." Nowadays we call the stallion a cowgirl—or, if you prefer, a reverse cowgirl—and the brothel is referred to as "Building Z." There are no rooms per se, just stones in the dusty ground, the outlines of what was once a place for sex and wine and song and human trafficking and slavery.

The archaeological museum is a large open area in the center of the sprawling modern metropolis, a short walk from the Acropolis and the ancient Agora. My guide to the Kerameikos was Nicolas Nicolaides, a historian, writer, and Ph.D. student as well as one of the cofounders of Big Olive, a company that offers cultural tours of Athens. He is something of an expert on the life of the city then and now, and, like most Athenians, he is an enthusiast for a good taverna. Almost all my favorite restaurants in Athens I discovered through him. He can be professorial when he's spouting information, but he is quick to smile and is prone to fits of giggles that remind me of a cartoon character.[*]

Nicolas pointed across the Kerameikos to a large pile of rocks in what looked like a vast pile of rocks. "The city gate, over there, you can see the steps and you can see the road in the middle." I looked, but I wasn't sure I was seeing it. From our vantage point the entire area was just a jumble of partial walls and outlines of buildings embedded in the dirt with a scattering of stones and ancient grave markers. Some of the markers were ornate, in the shape of virile animals like bulls or lions, while others depicted scenes of the dead being visited by their friends and family. My favorite was a simple marble slab from the fifth century BCE with the message I AM THE BOUNDARY MARKER OF THE SACRED WAY chiseled into it. Who says they didn't have street signs in antiquity?

The Kerameikos is the edge of classical Athens, just inside the city walls. It was where you entered and exited through a double-doored gate called the Dipylon. As Nicolas said, "You can imagine the products coming from either the countryside or the port of Piraeus. And the road would be lined with long buildings, lines of columns that would provide shade." If I squinted, I could see the ghosts of the towers that protected the Dipylon. Of course the towers were now just piles of wind-eroded stones under a corrugated plastic roof.

Nicolas continued to point out faint traces of the old city. "You can see the line starts near the oleander." And you could. It was the road that used to go out, past the city gates and the

---

[*] Specifically Dick Dastardly's sidekick, Muttley, from Hanna-Barbera's 1968 animated show *Wacky Races*.

cemetery, past Epicurus's garden, to Plato's Academy. I don't know how other tourists feel when they suddenly see the traces of the ancient world and get a whisper of what it must have been like so long ago, but for me I felt a strange sensation overtake me—I was moved, reader. Awestruck. Maybe I was dehydrated. It was a weird feeling, something that I think people call "spiritual." It reminded me of hiking the Incan trail to Machu Picchu with an Andean man, a historian and guide, who said he never got tired walking in the mountains because he got energy from Pachamama every time he walked the trail. For him it was spiritual. For me it was the coca leaves that kept me going. They say the spirit moves the Catholics who walk the Camino de Santiago and the Muslims on the hajj. That I had that kind of feeling in an area famous for ancient wine bars and whorehouses perhaps says more about me than I'd like to admit.

The author in the alley (*photograph by Diana Faust*).

Coming into the city, people would have seen the Acropolis on the hill, the fortified walls, and then passed through the gates and entered a bustling commercial area. Nicolas swept his hand across the map: "They were the brothels of the city of Athens, so we are on the edge of the city. It's interesting because even today, if you visit a European city, usually the brothels are around the train station or the port. It's where you enter the city. So here it was exactly the same."[1]

It's funny to think that areas like the Kerameikos become liminal spaces. Travelers enter a city and the threshold they cross is lined with brothels and taverns. Sex for hire and booze on tap—that's how weary travelers know they're back in civilization.

But now it's just rubble. We know Building Z was a brothel during the time Ariphrades was alive. So it's likely that I was standing in the exact location where Ariphrades excited the flute girls. Ground zero for comedic and cunnilingual notoriety.

Nicolas adjusted his baseball cap. "The deeper you get during an excavation, the further back you go in time, so if you try to read an archaeological site you see that sometimes buildings are built one on top of the other. That's what people did. If the buildings were destroyed by war or earthquake or anything, they would come back and build on top of the old buildings and the buildings of their ancestors. And what's interesting is they almost always used the same architectural materials, which is why the bottom layer is usually missing. The concept of preservation is something that comes with modernity. People would use anything, even statues and columns, as building materials."

And they did, dumping beautiful sculptures into the ground to build fortifications against the Persians or the Spartans or the Romans or whoever was attacking that week. It was a practical solution to a pressing problem. You simply use the materials on hand so you don't have to go all the way up to the mountain in order to extract marble. That's what happened to the Library of Hadrian, an exquisite temple of learning sacrificed to fortify the city walls. You can still see the ruins just off Monastiraki Square.

(*Photograph by C. Messier, Creative Commons*)

The other reason libraries and temples and public buildings are destroyed is power. Throughout its history the Christian church has used pagan or Mayan or whatever kind of temples it found and built on top of them, converting one kind of sacred space into its kind of sacred space. Churches might be places of worship, but they are also symbols of power. They became the dominant narrative, absorbing the old, appropriating pagan feast days and turning a harvest festival into Christmas, and recasting Greek and Roman deities as apostles. If they couldn't subsume it, they simply destroyed what they didn't like. Imagine if that constant ebb and flow of conquest and destruction hadn't happened? What if the dominant powers had allowed the past to continue to flourish alongside it?

But the Christians were insecure and destroyed what came before. I'm singling out Christianity because it is the dominant force in Greece, but this kind of behavior is practiced by almost all the major monotheistic religions. Perhaps it's simply what happens when your foundational beliefs are based on fiction.

I'm not an archaeologist. You don't see me down in a pit brushing dust off some crockery or spelunking for ancient treasures wearing a weather-beaten fedora. So why was I moved by this pile of rubble in the Kerameikos? So much about the ancient Athenian civilization is lost that most of what we have are gaps. As historian James N. Davidson writes, "While scholarly attention has been distracted elsewhere, some extraordinary gaps have been allowed to open up in our knowledge of ancient culture and society. The lack of work on Greek heterosexuality and (until recently and outside France) ancient food are particularly striking."[2]

Scholars do their best to try to figure out what life might have been like back then, but as we've seen, contemporary biases skew their conclusions. It's a lot of very highly educated guesses, filling the gaps with conjecture, sometimes wishful thinking, romanticized ideas, and political agendas. One of my favorites is the scholar who studied Athenian pottery and decided that the depictions of anal sex between two men weren't actually anal sex but something called "interfemoral intercourse." As Holt N. Parker writes, "So, just as a good girl in the 1950s might allow some 'heavy petting' without losing her reputation but would not 'go all the way,' so a good eromenos could allow interfemoral intercourse, but not penetration."[3] In other words they were rubbing their dicks between each other's thighs, because to actually penetrate another man would diminish his standing in Athenian society. But really, I'm not sure I buy it. It sounds like something that might happen at a church sleepaway camp and not what a penetration-obsessed society would do. Why wouldn't they just stick it in? They stuck it in everywhere else.

Aristophanes wrote jokes about buttfucking, but I can't find one about interfemoral intercourse. I don't mean to harsh a classicist's buzz. Academics can't help but inject their personal agenda into a reading of the ancients; they have to fill in the gaps with something. It's normal to try to connect with this ancient culture, to attempt to see it in terms we understand, namely, *our terms*. It's human nature. I'm totally supportive of this kind of speculation. As a writer, it's the gaps that interest me. The parts that were destroyed or suppressed or lost. If our imagination is our superpower—the thing that we believe separates us from other animals—then we can visualize and conceive of almost anything, from the pearly gates of Heaven and the fiery pits of Hell, to fantasy worlds with elves and sorcerers, to life on a space station, to what our boss looks like naked. We might not always get it right—in fact we often envision things that are impossible, entirely upside down—but our imagination fills in the gaps. When thinking about ancient Athens, the gaps are more like chasms and neglected areas of study. Just like underappreciated insects, orphan groups are everywhere.

Much of what we think we know about Athens comes from playwrights, poets, and shards of pottery, and it really begs the question: Just how reliable is it? Nowadays we hardly read anymore, let alone recite poetry or go to the theater. As talented as they are, would we want future humans to try to comprehend our civilization through the work of Louise Glück, Tennessee Williams, and some crockery from Ikea? Of course it'll be worse than that: two thousand years from now scholars will be studying fragments of *Iron Man 3* and *Avengers: Infinity War* and the various iterations of *Spiderman* and episodes of *The Apprentice*, wondering why we were so dumb and violent and what kind of pagan religion worshipped insect people. We will wish they had our poets and playwrights.

So what if your story is simply that you wrote some jokes, you made people laugh, you were engaged with your society and culture at the time, and you took as much pleasure in the world as you could? And after that, if your work disappears . . . well, does it matter? Not every writer gets a legacy that lasts thousands of years. Comedy is an in-the-moment kind of thing, it doesn't always travel well, and it often comes with an expiration date. The pleasures of writing humor come from taking chances, allowing yourself to be vulnerable, and mocking your own eccentricities, and that openness to all the foibles and pitfalls of your own humanity buys you some credit to poke holes in the hubris of the arrogant, the know-it-alls, the pious, and the dimwitted bosses who think they run the world. I can imagine Ariphrades was amused by the life he found himself living, the names he'd been called, the infamy he'd achieved. You learn to take your pleasures and your notoriety with some equanimity.

This must be what archaeologists feel when they start excavating a site or a classics professor might feel when she unrolls a newly discovered scroll. Are they excited by what they will find or what they imagine they might find? Is it like the jolt of brain chemicals we get when we gamble? Interestingly, it's not when we win but when the dice are rolling, when the flop is being laid down, when the slots are spinning, that the brain gets excited; it's the possibilities, the potential, the unknown about to be revealed, that turns us on. That's the thrill of excavation, the jazz of discovery.

There's not a lot of excavation in our modern lives; people don't dig very deep. The basic needs of living, the constant distractions of media and the internet, our desires and delusions— these are all glittering on the surface, and we rarely stop and take a moment and look at what's underneath. We don't think critically about information we've been given. We seem reluctant to peel back the layers or think about the gaps. But that's where our story is: buried underneath the debris and detritus of whatever system we are subscribing to, whether it's capitalism or Judaism, commercialism or Christianity, Buddhism or socialism, these systems are constructs to distract us from excavating our lives. They fill in the gaps with prefab dogma so we don't have to think about the unknowable or confront the mystery of life.

Being in Athens, thinking about the past, seeing the contrails of the ancient world, makes me want to think about things in a different way. What if we embraced the gaps? What if we left some mysteries mysterious? Because what does it say about our civilization that if something doesn't fit our current narrative, we destroy it? That can't be healthy. It creates cognitive dissonance. Isn't rewriting the past to fit what we want to believe the definition of borderline personality disorder? Why don't we put down our smartphones and turn off our televisions and really start looking at ourselves and our connection to the world? Can we trade superficial amusements for deeper pleasures? Can we live with gaps in what is and isn't knowable? Is civilization a kind of mental illness?

This is a book of questions. I'm sorry I don't have more answers.

Parabasis

In ancient Greek comedies the parabasis is a rant. A time-out. A space for the author to say a few words. Which is supposed to be different from the agon, where the characters do all the talking. Usually the parabasis divides the agon, giving the audience a little intermission from the main story. And, as I showed in previous chapters, the parabasis is where the author calls out people he or she doesn't like and holds them up for ridicule. I can only surmise that the comedy routines of Don Rickles and Triumph the Insult Comic Dog were inspired by this classic theatrical form. Who knew?

In the parabasis for *Wasps* Aristophanes berates the audience for failing to give *Clouds* the acclaim he felt it was due. He has the chorus tell the audience:

> *Last year you betrayed him beyond measure when he sowed*
> *some brand new ideas which failed to take root because you*
> *didn't understand them properly—although he swears by*
> *Dionysus over countless libations that no one has ever heard*
> *comic poetry better than that . . .*
> *But in the future, my good people,*
> *Cherish and nurture more*
> *Those poets who seek*
> *To say something new.*
> *Keep hold of their ideas*
> *And keep them in your clothes-boxes*
> *With the citrons.*
> *And if you do this, after a year*
> *Your cloaks*
> *Will smell of cleverness.*[1]

I love Aristophanes for that. It's just so audacious. Love me or you're stupid. I suppose there's something liberating about having an ego that supercharged. Whether it comes from a place of insecurity and rage or he's playing himself as a character who just does not give a fuck, either way it's remarkable. I can't imagine having the balls or the hubris to stand up and say something like that, and, to be perfectly honest, I want a clever-smelling jacket. So like my parodos at the beginning of this book, my parabasis will be a little different. I'm not going to call out local Angelenos and mock them—although Mayor Garcetti is certainly due a public ribbing for his fainthearted-ness in the face of multiple crises and sycophantic groveling to the powerful for a cushy job in Washington. But I'm not going to stoop to that. Let's keep it classy.

There's been a glut of books talking about the ancient world; some of them are self-help, some of them are philo-sophical inquiries using ancient texts to reframe the present. Recent titles like *How to Be an Epicurean: The Ancient Art of Living Well*, by Catherine Wilson; *Aristotle's Way: How Ancient Wisdom Can Change Your Life*, by Edith Hall; *The Stoic Challenge: A Philosopher's Guide to Becoming Tougher, Calmer, and More Resilient*, by William Irvine; *How to Think Like a Roman Emperor: The Stoic Philosophy of Marcus Aurelius*, by Donald Robertson; and *The Obstacle Is the Way: The Timeless Art of Turning Trials into Triumph*, by Ryan Holiday.

I think the original philosophers would be delighted to see their ideas back in circulation. So let me throw my hat in the ring. How about a little Ariphrades-inspired pleasure to improve your life? Or improve the life of someone you love? At the very least we can start dismantling the patriarchy, give women equal rights, and stand back while they take their fair share of, well, everything. They've earned it.

Of course pulling from the past to explain the present can have a dark side. Some ancient philosophers have been co-opted by the "alt-right" who—overlooking the sodomy and interfemoral intercourse—look back on ancient Greece as the good old days, when white dudes were the bosses of the world, enslaved human beings did the hard work, and women cooked, cleaned, and received regular deposits of semen without complaint. I suppose in their minds a few pull quotes from Socrates and a picture of the Parthenon spiff up their sulky resentment at being involuntarily celibate, lend gravitas to their misogynistic whining. But it's all so unearned. Like open carry permits and dressing up in camouflage, it's macho posturing from dudes who never learned to share, guys who think they deserve to be the boss because, well, that's what they think and their daddy promised them. As classicist Donna Zuckerberg writes in her excellent book on the topic of alt-right co-opting of the ancients, *Not All Dead White Men: Classics and Misogyny in the Digital Age*, "They idealize a model for gendered behavior that erases much of the social progress that has been achieved in the last two thousand years—and they are using ancient literature to justify it."[2] And if you point out that they're just cherry-picking the bits that bolster their racism and misogyny, they go on all-out social media rampages, as Zuckerberg discovered when she published an article critical of the Far Right's misreading of Stoic philosophy. As she writes in her book, "It shows that these men enjoy learning about the ancient world because they believe that they and the ancients share similar beliefs, and they think that anybody who is not as misogynistic and xenophobic as the Greeks and Romans must not truly appreciate and wish to preserve ancient literature and culture." Which in their minds is reason enough for posting death threats and rape fantasies. Since this is my parabasis, my stepping forward, let me be clear: *Those guys can go fuck themselves.*

Of course we know from Ariphrades's example that not all the Athenians felt the same way. In fact I would venture that there might have been more equality for women in ancient

Athens than we'll ever know, because so much of the written record was destroyed by dudes who wanted to keep women down and stay in power. The patriarchy protects the patriarchy. Haters gonna hate. Oligarchs gonna garch.

It's interesting that the alt-right hasn't taken to Epicurus. I guess his egalitarian philosophy of a life lived in pursuit of pleasure, with men and women sharing peace, poetry, and lentils, is a bit too hippie-dippie—not enough domination and forced penetration for the fascists.

Why are these books so popular? Maybe we relate to the ancients because they lived in an imperialist empire built on conquest, exploitation, enslavement, and constant war, and if we look in the mirror, don't we see the same thing? Has the world really changed? The ruthless extraction and destruction of the natural world, the profound abuses of workers while the oligarchs and Wall Street fat cats get richer and richer, the unending wars and the militarization of everything; it's all empire all the time. You can't go to a fucking baseball game without pledging allegiance to the American empire while armed soldiers parade the flag around and fighter jets zoom overhead. Really? Is this necessary? *It's a ball game.* But those in power control the story, and right now the story is one of fetishizing the military and the myth of the exceptional state. And this story of empire is as fictional as any novel. The reality of life in the United States and the myth they're selling have been drifting further and further apart for decades. There are gaps in the plot you could drive a truck through. What would happen if we stopped filling in the gaps with bullshit? Stopped echoing empty platitudes about making America great or the shining city on the hill or the only place where the free are truly free to freely . . . what? It's all propagandish sludge that we've been spoon-fed since birth. It's not true. Just open your eyes. The American empire is not exceptional. It's like every other empire that came before it. How long can we suspend our disbelief? So what if we just said no? What if we disrupted the current narrative, said no thank you to the militarization of everything, and yes to pleasure and shared humanity? Empires fall. It's what they do. It's what they always have done. Isn't it time we changed that by changing our consciousness? Isn't it time to make room for pleasure, the natural world, and a spirit of egalitarianism?

End parabasis.

This Library Is on Fire

As long as there has been written language, there has been a need for a place to store the writing. Typically it was the people in charge who kept the written word: documents were housed in palaces by the rulers, religious leaders stored scrolls and tablets in temples, wealthy elites stashed manuscripts in their homes, and schools and centers of learning held other important writing. Knowledge was power, and possessing the written word was evidence of that power.

The Sumerians were reported to have libraries as far back as 3400 BCE, and by the sixth century BCE libraries in ancient Greece were fairly common. In what still holds true today, you just weren't a proper city if you didn't have a public library.

Alexandria, the bustling port in Egypt, decided it wanted the best and biggest library in the world and set out to build it. At its height, in the third and second centuries BCE, the Great Library of Alexandria is reported to have held more than half a million scrolls. The majority of them were writings by Hellenistic, or Greek, writers. They included texts of philosophy, science, medicine, and, naturally, the tragedies and comedies of the Athenian stage.

Built during the reign of Ptolemy II Philadelphus (although the idea apparently came from his father, Ptolemy I Soter), the library was part of a larger center for learning dedicated to the Muses called the Mouseion—not to be confused with Disneyland. It became known for its aggressive acquisition of texts, buying other libraries and forcing visiting ships to surrender any scrolls they might have on board to be copied by the Mouseion scribes. Scholars received royal stipends and were encouraged to work on whatever projects excited them, creating one of the world's first think tanks. It didn't hurt that Alexandria was the hub of the papyrus industry; so anything scroll related went through Alexandria. Those really long books you had to read in high school, the *Odyssey* and the *Iliad*, you can thank the librarians of Alexandria for preserving Homer's epic poems.

Nineteenth-century rendering of the Library of Alexandria by O. Von Corven (*Wikimedia Commons*).

I wanted to figure out what might have happened to Ariphrades's work—and the work of so many Greek comedic writers of that time—so I turned to Matthew Battles, author of *Library: An Unquiet History* and *Palimpsest: A History of the Written Word*.[1] Matthew is the director of scholarly initiatives at Harvard University's metaLAB, which calls itself "an idea foundry, knowledge-design lab, and production studio experimenting in the networked arts and humanities," which sounds a bit like the ancient library at Alexandria. He's a handsome and slightly scruffy-looking hipster-philosopher who, when he's not writing books, is involved in projects that range from philosophical rumination on the dark power of the internet to devising ways we might turn invasive plant species into tasty desserts. In other words, he's the perfect person to talk to about Ariphrades and what might have happened to his plays.

"Written material was pretty ubiquitous in the ancient world. You saw it in ascriptions, you heard it read out in edicts and in announcements, but it was very difficult to produce and very difficult to share, and people shared it and people shed themselves of it for, I think, quite significant reasons. I mean, both getting rid of something or taking the trouble to produce it meant that there was significant cause. It wasn't ephemeral and disposable the same way that written materials feel to us now." Matthew paused before continuing. "For example a poet would often produce a poem in order to impress somebody, somebody who could be a patron or somebody to whom a favor was owed. Those are the kinds of moments that would cause a poem to be copied out. So only a very few copies would have ever existed in the first place."

But what about a bawdy comic play?

"Something that's perhaps salacious or risqué is less likely to be copied out by one of the slaves. I think you're probably more likely to just hide it away somewhere."

Which makes me think that men have been stashing porno mags under their mattresses since the written word began.

I mentioned Stephen Greenblatt's book *The Swerve: How the World Became Modern* and asked Matthew if the same kind of religion-inspired suppression of manuscripts might've happened to the ancient Greek writers.

As it turns out, this question is something Matthew has spent a lot of time thinking about. "Yeah, I think there are a lot of ways in which manuscript material survives and fails to survive in the ancient world. As you say about Lucretius, suppression is a big part of it. In fact, the Library of Alexandria really suffered its biggest losses not because of accidental fires by Julius Caesar or the invasion of the Muslims, but because Christians began to go through their iconoclastic* moment and took issue not only with certain aspects of knowledge that they thought were transgressive, but knowledge itself. Some of the ways in which these things survive are interesting and I think provide a whole series of mishaps and near misses over the long sweep of time, that at any one point of which work could be snuffed out."

I was not raised in the Judeo-Christian tradition. When I was growing up the only religion my family belonged to was the Kansas City Chiefs and our sacrament was Ruffles potato chips and Dr Pepper, although on special occasions my mother would buy a strange sour cream–based clam dip that she liked. We didn't believe in god, even though the Chiefs won the Super Bowl in 1970. I was never molested by a priest or forced to handle snakes, so I have nothing personal against organized religion. But as an outsider looking in, as an observer surveying the catastrophic damage wrought throughout history by people obsessed with forcing their beliefs on everyone else, I can say with confidence that the world would be a better place without it.

It is well documented that for much of our history organized religion has tried to destroy anything to do with sexuality, sexual liberation, and equal rights for women, so it doesn't seem so far-fetched to think that they might've chucked scrolls of smutty and irreverent Greek comedies into the fireplace. I asked Matthew how pervasive he thought this Christian suppression was.

"Oh, it had quite a strong effect, and it reached very deep into the written record of the ancient world. That's a very real

---

* Around 726 BCE the Byzantine emperor Leo III banned all religious icons and images in the Christian churches, which resulted in widespread destruction of sculptures, paintings, texts, etcetera. It is also where we get the word "iconoclasm," which is from the Greek for "breaker of icons."

force affecting the preservation of these works. I would say that there were other forces as well, and it's interesting to think about some cults or schools of thought that might also have made somebody get rid of work or made somebody fear being discovered to have work. Stoicism, in particular, was a philosophical tradition that had a certain kind of moral . . ." He hesitated to find the right word before he said, "It tended to stick its nose up in the air."

The Stoics were resolute funwreckers: anti-pleasure, anti-sexual adventuring, anti-everything Epicurus stood for. They were all about virtue and logic and not letting desires influence your decisions—like a philosophy founded by the Starfleet science officer Spock. It's easy to imagine the Stoics, Christians, and Vulcans disapproving of Ariphrades, albeit for different reasons. Matthew agreed. "Literature largely circulated among the elite, and these are very risk-averse people. Even though it's the world from which we draw our Western intellectual traditions, and the concept of the liberal arts in particular, we call them that because they're about books, but also because they're about the arts of free people, the knowledge forms of free people. That freedom was something that you got by birthright or you got by having somebody buy it for you. It was not a universal commodity."

Nowadays we might call that "privilege." And certainly there was a class dynamic in whose plays were produced and who was entitled to express their point of view on the Athenian stage. I'm not sure things have changed that much—who is given the authority to speak has always depended on class, status, and the approval of the moneyed elite and those in power—although social media has opened the doors for a multitude of voices to sound off.

The writings of the ancient Greeks were either scratched into clay or written out on papyrus scrolls. These early scrolls looked sort of like a pirate map you might see in a movie. In his book *Bookrolls and Scribes in Oxyrhynchus*, Duke University professor and member of the American Society of Papyrologists William A. Johnson describes the dimensions of an ancient scroll as roughly eight to ten inches wide and up to twelve inches in diameter—about the same size as one of Yotam Ottolenghi's cookbooks—and up to thirty-six feet long when unrolled.[2] Their weight depended on the quality of the papyrus, naturally. In many ways scrolls were more cumbersome and more delicate than the later codex, which became what we now call a book.

Matthew continued: "It's interesting to think about how these things get transmitted, and it's hard for us, I think, to imagine what a world is like where everything is a manuscript, right? There's no press. There's no stamping these things out. If you wanted to disseminate your work you had to figure out ways to disseminate it. You had to write a lot of copies of it and put them into the hands of important people, and it helped to have slaves too." He paused for a moment then added, "Which militates against the democratic origins of comedy to a certain extent, and yet it's definitely in the mix."

Copies of these works were rare, yet most Greek cities had libraries and many wealthy Athenians maintained private collections. A good example of this is the private library at Herculaneum in what is now Italy. It once held a massive collection of Greek manuscripts, which were destroyed when Mount Vesuvius erupted in 79 CE. Almost two thousand carbonized scrolls have been recovered, and although they look like barbecued dinosaur turds, scientists are finding ways to read them through something called "x-ray phase-contrast tomography," which is like a CT scan. One of the pleasant surprises from this research is the uncovering of several Epicurean texts written by Philodemus, one of Epicurus's disciples.

I'm holding out hope that one of Ariphrades's plays might be among the carbonized husks entombed in the library. But it leads me to wonder, with all these public and private libraries everywhere, you would think more of these works would have survived. So what happened?

Matthew had an answer. "It can be big events, like the shifts in religion or in cults, in political regime, but it can also be that just somebody falls out of favor, and you don't want to have that work around anymore. Or an individual who has got some of this work falls out of favor and gets rid of something in order to make things right."

Or maybe a second-century Marie Kondo decided the scrolls no longer "spark joy."

Matthew laughed. "There are also interesting ways that things might survive and still never come to light. Two of the major ways in which—and I write about one and a half of these in *Library*, because I spent a lot of time in *Library: An Unquiet History* looking at the genizah, which is a repository for discarded manuscript materials in synagogues. They were usually a separate room. They could be as simple as a hole in the floor, but typically they were a room that was walled up except for one hole, and you'd literally push pieces of written material through that hole, and they'd fall into this room that nobody had access to, because there's no door to it. You'd have to break a wall or go through the hole to get at the stuff in there. And this was done because of prescriptions in Judaism, which were quite common in the times [and] still exist in orthodox communities, against destroying written material because it might have the secret name of god in it. So this taboo was quite strong, particularly in the ancient world, and all of these written materials that were being discarded, they could be things like letters, they could be things like shopping lists. Quite literally, it was the whole range of written material. They'd get pushed into these genizahs, and there they would stay for a long time."

I had never heard of genizahs until I'd encountered Matthew's work, but, simply put, they are storage areas and repositories for texts that come in all shapes and sizes, from an ancient cave in Israel to a modern-day collection container that looks like a drive-through book drop at your local library. There are times when my home office resembles a crude genizah.

"The most famous of these was one in the Grand Temple in Cairo that was broken into in the late nineteenth century during the British rule of Egypt. These papyrus manuscripts began to get out onto the market, and papyrologists and classicists began to hear that people were selling these things that were manuscripts, fragments of manuscripts that nobody had ever seen before. And so the Cairo genizah ends up furnishing this enormous trove of materials, some of which was material that was known material that was lost. And some of it was brand-new material. It included letters by Maimonides, and lots of fragments of Talmudic texts, and differing interpretations of Torah texts that have passed out of understanding. Also, just lots of demotic stuff, like I said earlier, like the proverbial shopping list, or a recipe, or even things like charms or potions would get written down and pushed into the genizah.

"Also, a lot of material ended up in trash middens, just in garbage dumps, and particularly stuff that was written on ostraca, these fragments of clay that people would use as a notepad. I mean, writing material itself was hard to come by, and it was usually much easier to just take a broken pot and scratch characters in it than it was to kind of go through the trouble and expense of procuring or making papyrus, or other later forms of writing medium like parchment. So people would throw these things away, and, again in Egypt, there's a famous trove of papyri, fragments of written material, and ostraca from this town called Oxyrhynchus, which is like the 'town of the short-nosed fish,' up the river along the Nile. And that has included some fragments of literary works that had gone missing or had been forgotten."

And what might've happened to one of Ariphrades's plays? Matthew had a thought. "It's fun to imagine a kid having a little mini-genizah of his own under his bed, where salacious material ends up so that his parents' slaves can't find it."

I love the idea of someone secretly reading Ariphrades— much like someone might read *Mad Magazine*, or a graphic novel by Alison Bechdel, or one of the banned novels by Kathy Acker or William Burroughs. Whether they're Christian or Stoics or Islamists or concerned parents, the morality police haven't stopped trying to ban books and suppress ideas that challenge the status quo, especially when it concerns sexuality. What does it say about a supposedly free society when one of the most challenged and banned books of the last decade is a picture book about homosexual penguins?[3] This isn't about protecting the children any more than denying women reproductive freedom is about being pro-life; it's about controlling the story. The Nazis burned books they deemed degenerate, the People's Republic of China torches books that are anti-communist, Tipper Gore founded the Parents Music Resource Center to advocate putting warning labels on music after she caught her daughter listening to a Prince song, rednecks drove their pickup trucks over Dixie Chick CDs because the women in the band (now known simply as "the Chicks") spoke out against the Iraq War, the Taliban blew up giant statues of Buddha in Afghanistan, and Christians have been burning books ever since they figured out how to light a fire. These are all examples of one group or another trying to impose its story, its narrative, on everyone else by destroying anything that runs counter to it. There's no nuance in a bonfire. Even parents of students at my old high school in Shawnee Mission, Kansas, took a book about a lesbian relationship called *Annie on My Mind*, by Nancy Garden, and burned it outside the school district's office. I'm guessing they didn't see the parallel between what they were doing and the Third Reich.

Somehow fragments of ancient stories survived, including these raunchy, phallus-toting-Satyr bits and pieces from various writers and various plays over the ages. The thing that I find fascinating about Ariphrades is that a writer as important as Aristotle was still talking about his work and yet we don't even have a fragment. He was eradicated. To me that's a signal that he was important in some way we don't understand. Maybe he was just popular.

Matthew agreed: "A kind of guilty pleasure and a box office hit."

"Exactly," I replied.

"And this is where this kind of issue of the rarity of manuscript materials becomes interesting. Again, only a very few copies might have supported that frequent performance of work. So somebody could be a big box office hit and be very rarely copied out."

Writers write to communicate ideas and emotions, to entertain and hopefully get people to think and feel more deeply. But for the most part they are writing for the present, for the society they live in. Writing is a real be-here-now kind of endeavor. At least for me anyway.

I don't think anyone writes with the idea that a hundred years after publication, he or she will still be in print or widely read. One hundred years ago people were reading Colette and D. H. Lawrence, Virginia Woolf and F. Scott Fitzgerald. These works still resonate with readers, but the bestselling books of 1921, according to *Publishers Weekly*, were by Sinclair Lewis, Dorothy Canfield, and Zane Grey. Other books in the 1921 top ten bestseller list include works by not exactly household names: Edith M. Hull, Mary Roberts Rinehart, Gertrude Atherton, and Coningsby Dawson.

Two hundred years ago you also had books like Mary Ann Kelty's *The Favourite of Nature* and George Matcham's *Anecdotes of a Croat*, both published in 1821 and all but unknown today.

Go back five hundred years and you start bumping up against books like Niccolò Machiavelli's *The Art of War* and John Skelton's *The Tunnyng of Elynour Rummyng*. Also a surprising number of poets who were burned at the stake.

In 1021 you might find a fresh copy of *The Tale of Genji*, by Murasaki Shikibu, and *Book of Optics*, by Arab mathematician Abū ʿAlī al-Ḥasan Ibn al-Haytham.

Because Matthew Battles is also an author, dipping his toes into the continuum of writers and writing, I asked him what he thought about legacy.

"I do think about that quite a bit myself. I think, with my own work, I feel like there are certain things, certain aspects of the pursuit, of some kind of writerly impact that have been constant throughout, but some of them have changed their valence or intensity. I certainly was driven by the thought of being remembered and being remembered a certain kind of way, but it's become increasingly more important to me to just do the work and to enjoy the momentary satisfaction that comes with whatever kind of magic happens, occasionally as it does."

This is excellent advice. Just do the work, even if doing the work is sometimes fraught. I'm not sure that people understand that it takes a degree of courage, a willingness to be vulnerable and expose yourself, when you publish a book.

Turning back to Ariphrades, Matthew said, "It's interesting to start to think about how somebody, particularly in these ancient milieus, would think about fame and memory."

I'm not sure that Ariphrades thought that Aristophanes's plays would still be performed two thousand years later, that his own legacy would be to be mocked as a besotted debauchee for thousands of years, but I wonder what he might've said if he did. Would he care? Would it have altered what he wrote or how he behaved?

Matthew understood what I was saying. "I got a rite of passage bad review in the *New York Times* a few years ago, and it was very ad hominem and clearly the guy—who I knew from some professional networks—had it out for me in a way that I was not anticipating. It struck me in the wake of that that the people whose work matters the most to me, like Borges, or Virginia Woolf, or certainly Poe . . . any literary figure has had people who absolutely hated them. And you have to risk that, right? In fact, it's almost like de rigueur. If you're going to have any kind of literary success, you're gonna have to suck in the minds of many people. And taking that on was something I didn't really think about too much when I got into this game."

I could not agree more with his assessment. Writers have to be brave and throw it down on the page. Which is why, throughout history, they have been imprisoned, burned at the stake, exiled, murdered. Of course that all changes when, instead of being remembered as a writer, Ariphrades is remembered for his sexual proclivities.

Matthew agreed. "Yeah, I mean, that's interesting because it raises the specter of somebody who's transgressive in a way that's ontologically or existentially threatening, not just somebody who's irritating in some way, but somebody who's very . . ."

He paused to consider what he was saying.

"I mean these are things that matter to us about latter-day figures, like Elton John. Somebody who scared people by a certain kind of flamboyance, a certain kind of sexual persona. And what's interesting about this world is that some elements of that sexual ontology are familiar and persist to this day, and some of them are so different from what we are used to. What's so intriguing about this case is that, in a sense, being submissive with or for a woman in the ancient world was queer, where today it could be a fetish or simply being a good partner. So the whole matrix of some elements of queerness and normativity are rearranged in surprising ways."

What Matthew calls "queerness," the transgressive challenging of cultural and societal norms through sexuality, might be the only legacy Ariphrades leaves us.

Maybe that's enough.

Ta Kanaria

Ta Kanaria is a taverna in Metaxourgeio. It's decidedly old school, a funky space with mismatched wooden tables and chairs, a checkerboard floor, and random art on the walls. It is both clean and dusty. It's not a tourist spot, it's a ramshackle neighborhood joint that's comfortable and familiar, like a baggy, moth-eaten sweater that you just can't throw away because it makes you feel good when you put it on.

(*Photograph courtesy of the author*)

In the afternoon, after the lunch rush, the usual suspects congregate. Inside, locals play dominoes and drink coffee, smoke cigarettes and shoot the breeze; outside, people sit in the sun reading, maybe writing in a notebook. Couples chat. Sometimes someone pulls out a guitar and plays a song or two.

But mostly the music is on the sound system, a loud and eclectic mix of guitar rock, heavy metal, and blues. It's not unusual to hear Reverend Horton Heat and Black Sabbath followed by Muddy Waters and PJ Harvey. The food isn't fancy, just simple salads, bowls of olives, and assorted snacks; but it's fresh and tasty. The beer is cold and the wine is cheap. What's not to love? It is one of Diana and my favorite places in Athens and where we often ended up after a night out, getting one last drink and maybe some eggplant spread and rusks before going to bed.

Most of the staff look like the customers, as if neighbors started handing out menus or got behind the counter and whipped up some sandwiches. Maybe they are. For all I know Ta Kanaria could be an anarchist small plates collective.

One afternoon we sat down for lunch. Our waiter was slightly older than the others, brawny and compact, his arms covered in tattoos. He was wearing a faded Led Zeppelin tour T-shirt, and for a moment I thought it might be possible he'd been a roadie on one of their tours. He handed us menus and right away I noticed a large *Ace of Spades* tattoo on his forearm. I pointed and said, "Motörhead?"

He smiled and said, "Classic."

There were only a couple of other tables inside, so he put the Beatles' "I Want You (She's So Heavy)" on the sound system and turned it up. Outside the taverna it was hot, the midday sun was frying the city, but inside it was dark and the sultry sound of electric guitars softened the day. A pitcher of cold white wine arrived. We relaxed.

This taverna would've been on the path between Plato's Academy and the city gates, and it's entirely possible that Ariphrades and his brothers might have stopped for a drink somewhere right around here. I imagine he would've needed a drink to settle his nerves because—in an entirely fictional flashback—tonight was his big night.

Ariphrades looked away from the stage and across the theater toward the rows in front. He could see the judges from his vantage point, their shoulders shaking with laughter, their heads thrown back in howls of delight. They were drunk, no doubt, but they were watching his play and they were obviously enjoying it. He felt a tap on his arm and turned to see his father decant some wine into a cup and hand it to him. Automenes smiled and leaned into Ariphrades. "I think you have a hit." Ariphrades took the cup and forced himself to have a sip. He hoped his father was right.

From the looks of it, it was a success. The theater was packed, people who couldn't get a seat were standing on the sides and at the top. Best of all, everyone was laughing, enjoying the performance. He saw Leogoras pounding his knee and howling at a joke. His patron turned and caught his eye and gave him an encouraging nod.

Phoenician Kisses was his best work, he knew it. He took another sip of wine. It was good, but he was too nervous to enjoy it. He turned his attention to the stage, where the Poet, now dressed as a woman, was begging Priapus to restore his manhood. The actor playing the god was dressed in a costume with an outlandish seven-foot-long phallus, which he used to hilarious effect, banging into the chorus, knocking over props, and clobbering the Poet.

> POET: *I was once the greatest writer alive!*
> PRIAPUS: *We know. You told us. Repeatedly. But look at the bright side! Now you can receive more than just the praise of your admirers, now you can take their semen! Much better than a pat on the back.*
> [The Poet falls to his knees and begins sobbing.]
> PRIAPUS: *See! You're already getting the hang of being a woman.*
> POET: *Help me! Please! I'll do anything!*

[Priapus considers it.]
PRIAPUS: There is a way to reverse the spell.
POET: Anything.
PRIAPUS: I'm not sure you're up for it.
POET: I have no penis!
PRIAPUS: Don't get testy.
POET: I am a woman! Wouldn't that make you angry?
[Priapus waves his giant phallus around the stage.]
PRIAPUS: I like women. All of them.

Ariphrades leaned forward in his seat. This was his favorite part of the play. He watched as Priapus swung his massive cock around in a circle. He then stopped, the phallus pointed directly at the Poet.

PRIAPUS: To become a man, you must lick the hot spot of every flute girl in the city.
POET: What?

The audience howled with laughter. They had been going to the theater for years and knew exactly who the joke was on.

PRIAPUS: You heard me.
POET: That is not how you become a man. That is the opposite of being a man.
PRIAPUS: Suit yourself.

Priapus left the stage, and the chorus came on to convince the Poet of the joys of being a woman. Their examples were, naturally, scathingly sarcastic, poking fun at the patriarchs of the city and their treatment of women. But as the Poet slowly realized that he must go on a quest to lick every flute girl's hot spot, the chorus burst into song, an ode to something that couldn't be named, a celebration of pleasuring women, a rebuke to the narrow-mindedness of the naysayers. Like the title of the play, Ariphrades called the song "Phoenician Kisses." It was a showstopper.

Ariphrades was delighted to see the audience cheering the singers and laughing along with the lyrics. Some drunken revelers in the stands stood up and danced in place. It seemed as if everyone in Athens, the entire city, was cheering. He looked around to see if he could catch Aristophanes's reaction, but his shiny bald head was nowhere in sight.

I know it's a bit of a Hollywood ending, but I wanted to give Ariphrades a win. Not that he won the festival that year, that's too contrived, but he won the hearts and funny bones of his fellow Athenians. I think for him that was enough, even if posterity and decades of scholarship from historians might think otherwise. Would the world be different if the comedies of Ariphrades had survived? Who can say? What if his habit of pleasuring women had become popular back in the day? Would equality in sexual pleasure equal equality in society?

Imagine a world where men and women are equals. It embarrasses me to acknowledge that in 2020 the U.S. government has still not passed the Equal Rights Amendment. Is it really so difficult to give women equal rights? I mean . . . seriously? And while the patriarchy controls the story for now, there are gaps, opportunities for an alternative interpretation. The treatment of women, the injustice toward people of color, the economic terrorism of the corporate class. These are all cracks in a patriarchal system of oppression, and with enough pressure that crack can turn into a fissure, a fissure that becomes a fracture that brings the whole rotten construct down. I believe it can happen. Because consciousness is not static, it moves forward.

Would it matter if the narrative were reframed? If we realized that patriarchy is no way to live in the world? Professor Hanink has a thought: "It matters because ideas about what antiquity really means—and controversies over who owns its legacy—have played an enormous role in shaping the West's sense of its civilizational roots."[1]

I agree. I think we all know who claims the legacy, but I'm not sure we've gotten the whole story. There are so many gaps, and they've been filled by men in power with their own biases and agendas. Like in Philip K. Dick's novel *The Man in the High Castle*, you start to wonder which story is real. It's time we changed it up.

Have you ever noticed that the opening riff and the closing riff of "I Want You (She's So Heavy)" seamlessly connect back to each other? I did. Because the song had been playing for so long that Diana pulled out her phone and looked up how long the song actually was—seven minutes and forty-seven seconds as it turns out. We were now into some strange half-hour version of the song. Every time it looped back on itself we were surprised, like we were in a Möbius strip of "I Want You (She's So Heavy)." I looked across the taverna and saw that another couple had noticed the same thing.

Maybe I'm giving Ariphrades too much credit. Perhaps his plays were aimed at the lowest common denominator, like a classical *Jackass: The Movie.* We'll never know, but I'm willing to give him the benefit of the doubt. He was subjected to some of the most public of public ridicule that a person could endure and Aristophanes tried to cancel him repeatedly, but he kept on keeping on, a thorn in Aristophanes's side for more than thirty years.

It's time to reclaim his story and revive the Epicurean pursuit of pleasure. Instead of Stoicism and militarism, how about some sex and comedy? And while we're at it, why don't we let the Greek people decide what's best for themselves and their history? We act like we own that civilization. We don't. If anything the West has exploited it, performing some kind of narrative jiujitsu.

After forty minutes, or just over five repetitions of "I Want You (She's So Heavy)," we were laughing so hard that Diana had tears streaming down her cheeks. The other couple in the restaurant were howling, as if it were the single funniest thing ever. The waiter was oblivious, carrying on with his work, futzing around in the kitchen, taking plates to people eating on the sidewalk. Although I did notice his coworker glaring at him, an astonished expression on her face as the song began once again.

Why does Ariphrades's story matter? Because creativity matters. Desire matters. Making an effort matters. The world needs people like Ariphrades, people who aren't afraid to challenge the aristocracy, the ruling class, the status quo; people who have the potential to change the way people live. We need to cultivate enthusiasms like his. We need more people to go down on each other. In a speech to the European Congress of Ethnic Religions, Greek writer Vlassis Rassias said, "We reclaim the European identity. We reclaim our true value systems and our true ways. Our purpose is clear, to restore the once defeated[,] but not extinct, cultures of joy, freedom, polytheism, dignity, piety and uprightness, and, being a Hellene, please let me [add] of reason, humanism, eunomia and polyarchy."[2] Joy. Freedom. Humanism. I can get behind these. Let's stop being so cynical and greedy, have a little faith in each other, and bring about a more creative world.

As Henry Miller said so well:

> To live creatively, I have discovered, means
> to live more and more unselfishly, to live
> more and more *into* the world, identifying
> oneself with it and thus influencing it at

the core, so to speak. Art, like religion, it
now seems to me, is only a preparation, an
initiation into the way of life. The goal is
liberation, freedom, which means assuming
greater responsibility. To continue writing
beyond the point of self-realization seems
futile and arresting. The mastery of any form
of expression should lead inevitably to the
final expression—mastery of life.[3]

After eight repetitions—sixty-two solid minutes—of "I
Want You (She's So Heavy)," the waiter finally went to the
stereo and put on something else. I was so relieved that it
stopped that I can't remember what he played next. I do remember that the taverna burst into applause. The waiter
looked at us sheepishly. His coworker scowled and said, "Did
you have that on repeat?" He shrugged and said, "I like it."

As simple as that. Mastery of life.

The chorus leaves the stage.

Acknowledgments

I want to thank all the classicists, scholars, and translators who did the heavy lifting that made this book possible.

Much gratitude to the people who lent their voices to this project.

In Athens: Tilemachos Aidinis, Dimitra Papadopoulou, George Papamattheakis, Nicolas Nicolaides, Yanis Varoufakis, Evangelia Tseliou, Greg Prassas, Michalis Leontios, and Maria Panagiotopoulou and Olga Pavlatos of the Athens & Epidaurus Festival.

In the U.S.: Brian Brown, Matthew Battles, Mary Norris, James Romm, and Mark Anderson.

This book would not have been possible without the intelligence, enthusiasm, and courage of the great team at the Unnamed Press: Olivia Taylor Smith, Chris Heiser, Jaya Nicely, Kelsey Nolan, and ace copyeditor Nancy Tan.

A shout-out to my long-suffering agents: Mary Evans. Brian Lipson. Michèle Kanonidis.

A round of drinks to my colleagues who listened to me talk about this book for the past few years: David L. Ulin, Viet Thanh Nguyen, Liska Jacobs, Edan Lepucki, Laila Lalami, Tony Dushane, Jamison Stoltz, Adam Davidson, Chad Gomez Creasey, and Tod Goldberg.

And thanks to my friends and family for their continued support: Diana Faust, Jules Haskell Smith, Vincent Willems, Bruce and Cynthia Faust, Jennifer Matthews, and Santiago Gallego Villa.

Endnotes

An Introductory Scene

1. Diogenes Laertius, *Lives of Eminent Philosophers*, translated by R. D. Hicks (Cambridge, MA: Harvard University Press, 1931).

2. For more on Epicurus, I recommend Catherine Wilson's *How to Be an Epicurean: The Ancient Art of Living Well* (New York: Basic Books, 2019).

3. James Davidson, *Courtesans and Fishcakes: The Consuming Passions of Classical Athens* (New York: St. Martin's Press, 1998).

At the Symposium

1. Plato, *Symposium*, translated by Alexander Nehamas and Paul Woodruff (Indianapolis, IN: Hackett, 1989).

2. Jeffrey Rusten, ed., *The Birth of Comedy: Texts, Documents, and Art from Athenian Comic Competitions, 486–280* (Baltimore, MD: Johns Hopkins University Press, 2011).

3. "Platonius, *On the Distinctions among Comedies*," Living Poets, 2014 https://livingpoets.dur.ac.uk/w/Platonius,_On_the_Distinctions_among_Comedies_I.

4. W. J. W. Koster, trans., *Prolegomena de Comoedia* (Groningen, Netherlands: Bouma's, 1975).

Athens™®

1. Johanna Hanink, *The Classical Debt: Greek Antiquity in an Era of Austerity* (Cambridge, MA: Belknap Press, 2017).

2. Demosthenes, *Against Neaera*, translation by Norman W. DeWitt, Ph.D., and Norman J. DeWitt, Ph.D. (Cambridge, MA: Harvard University Press; London: William Heinemann Ltd. 1949.)

3. Xenophon, *Memorabilia,* translated by Amy L. Bonnette (Ithaca: Cornell University Press, 1994)

4. James Miller, *Examined Lives: From Socrates to Nietzsche* (New York: Farrar, Straus, Giroux, 2011)

5. David Kawalko Roselli, *Theater of the People: Spectators and Society in Ancient Athens* (Austin: University of Texas Press, 2011).

6. H. W. Fowler and F. G. Fowler, trans., *The Works of Lucian of Samosata* (Oxford: Clarendon Press, 1905).

7. Ian C. Storey, ed. and trans., *Fragments of Old Comedy*, vol. 2, Loeb Classical Library (Cambridge, MA: Harvard University Press, 2011).

The Case against Ariphrades

1. Aristophanes, *Clouds; Women in Power; Knights,* translated by Kenneth McLeish (Cambridge: Cambridge University Press, 1979).

2. Aristophanes, *The Complete Plays,* translated by Paul Roche (New York: New American Library, 2005).

3. Aristophanes, *Knights,* translated by J. Henderson, Loeb Classic Library (Cambridge, MA: Harvard University Press, 1998)

4. Karl Friedrich Forberg, *Manual of Classical Erotology (De figuris Veneris),* (Germany: 1824) Trans. Unknown (Manchester: Privately printed for Viscount Julian Smithson and friends, 1884)

5. Benjamin Dann Walsh, trans., *The Acharnians, Knights, and Clouds,* by Aristophanes (London: Henry G. Bohn, 1848).

6. Robert C. Bartlett, *Against Demagogues: What Aristophanes Can Teach Us about the Perils of Populism and the Fate of Democracy* (Berkeley: University of California Press, 2020).

7. Aristophanes, *Wasps,* translated by Alan H. Sommerstein (Warminster, UK: Aris & Phillips, 1983).

8. Aristophanes, *Wasps,* translated by Moses Hadas, in *The Complete Plays of Aristophanes,* edited by Moses Hadas (New

York: Bantam Books, 1962), 165–212.

9. Aristotle, *Politics and Poetics,* translated by Benjamin Jowett and H.S. Butcher (New York: The Heritage Press, 1964)

10. Aristophanes, *Peace,* translated by B. B. Rogers, in *The Complete Plays of Aristophanes,* edited by Moses Hadas (New York: Bantam, 1962), 213–62.

11. Aristophanes, *Women of the Assembly,* translated by Aaron Poochigian (New York: Liveright, 2021)

12. Found in the section "Dubiously Attributed Fragments" in Jeffrey Henderson, ed. and trans., *Aristophanes: Fragments,* Loeb Classic Library (Cambridge, MA: Harvard University Press, 2007).

13. Alan H. Sommerstein, "How to Avoid Being a *Komodoumenos,*" *Classical Quarterly* 46, no. 2 (1996): 327–56.

The Defense of Ariphrades

1. Mary Norris, *Greek to Me: Adventures of the Comma Queen* (New York: W. W. Norton, 2019).

2. Mary Norris, *Between You & Me: Confessions of a Comma Queen* (New York: W. W. Norton, 2015).

3. Aristotle, *The Poetics of Aristotle: Translation and Commentary,* translated by Stephen Halliwell (Chapel Hill: University of North Carolina Press, 1987).

4. Ian C. Storey, ed. and trans., *Fragments of Old Comedy,* vol. 1, Loeb Classical Library (Cambridge, MA: Harvard University Press, 2011).

5. Barry S. Strauss, *Fathers and Sons in Athens: Ideology and Society in the Era of the Peloponnesian War* (London: Routledge, 1993).

6. Joseph Roisman, *The Rhetoric of Manhood: Masculinity in the Attic Orators* (Berkeley: University of California Press, 2005).

7. Demosthenes, *Against Aristogeiton I,* translated by Joseph Roisman, *The Rhetoric of Manhood* (Berkeley: University of California Press, 2005)

8. Dean Obeidallah, "Why Are Conservatives So Freaked Out by Gays?," *Daily Beast*, March 1, 2014, https://www.thedaily-beast.com/why-are-conservatives-so-freaked-out-by-gays.

9. Stephen Greenblatt, *The Swerve: How the World Became Modern* (New York: W. W. Norton, 2012).

Amazonon Street

1. Henry Miller, *The Colossus of Maroussi* (San Francisco: Colt Press, 1941).

2. "Remarks by M. Centeno Following the Eurogroup Meeting of 21 June 2018," European Council, Council of the European Union, https://www.consilium.europa.eu/en/press/press-releases/2018/06/22/remarks-by-m-centeno-following-the-eurogroup-meeting-of-21-june-2018/.

3. Venetia Rainey, "Greece Exits Bailout, but 'Shackles and the Asphyxiation Continue,'" *The World*, August 20, 2018, https://www.pri.org/stories/2018-08-20/greece-exits-bail-out-shackles-and-asphyxiation-continue.

4. "The Burden of Disease in Greece, Health Loss, Risk Factors, and Health Financing, 2000–16: An Analysis of the Global Burden of Disease Study 2016," *Lancet Public Health* 3, no. 8 (August 2018): e395–406, http://dx.doi.org/10.1016/S2468-2667(18)30130-0.

5. Yanis Varoufakis, *Adults in the Room: My Battle with the European and American Deep Establishment* (New York: Farrar, Straus and Giroux, 2017).

6. Kerin Hope, "Greece Brain Drain Hampers Recovery from Economic Crisis," *Financial Times*, August 15, 2018, https://www.ft.com/content/24866436-9f9f-11e8-85da-eeb7a9ce36e4.

7. ZZ Packer, "Sarah Cooper Doesn't Mimic Trump. She Exposes Him," *New York Times*, June 25, 2020.

8. Daniel Lipman, "Trump says he plans to ban Tik Tok in the U.S." *Politico*, July 31, 2020 https://www.politico.com/news/2020/07/31/trump-plans-to-ban-tiktok-389956

9. From the Bhaddekaratta Sutta.

Rusk Never Sleeps
1. Attributed to Borges in Alastair Reid, "Neruda and Borges," *New Yorker*, June 24, 1996, as well as in Talk of the Town, *New Yorker*, July 7, 1986.

The Name of the Moth
1. Frederick DuCane Godman and Osbert Salvin, eds., *Biologia Centrali-Americana: Zoology, Botany, and Archaeology* (London: R. H. Porter, 1879–1915).
2. I also found the name in Ian W. B. Nye's doorstopper of a book *The Generic Names of Moths of the World*, vol. 1, *Noctuoidea: Noctuidae, Agaristidae, and Nolidae* (London: Trustees of the British Museum [Natural History], 1975).
3. *Ariphrades setula* (Noctuoidea: Noctuidae: Hypeninae).

The Antagonist of the Piece
1. Translated by Jeffery Henderson in Rusten, *The Birth of Comedy*.
2. Aristophanes, *Peace,* translated by Paul Roche (New York: New American Library, 2005)
3. Aristophanes, *Wasps*.
4. Ibid.
5. Kenneth McLeish in his translation notes in *Clouds; Women in Power; Knights,* by Aristophanes (Cambridge: Cambridge University Press, 1979).
6. From Lil Wayne's song "What's Wrong With Them," *I Am Not a Human Being* (Cash Money, 2010).
7. Rusten, *The Birth of Comedy*.
8. Lucian, *The Dead Come to Life or The Fisherman* translated by A.M. Harmon (London: William Heinemann, Ltd Cambridge: Harvard University Press 1925)
9. Storey, *Fragments of Old Comedy*, vol. 2.

10. Aristotle, *Constitution of the Athenians* 28.3. translated by H. Rackham. (Cambridge, MA, Harvard University Press; London, William Heinemann Ltd. 1952.)

11. Aristophanes, *Clouds, Women at the Thesmophoria, Frogs: A Verse Translation, with Introduction and Notes*, translated by Stephen Halliwell (Oxford: Oxford University Press, 2015).

12. Plato, *Plato in Twelve Volumes*, vol. 3, translated by W. R. M. Lamb (Cambridge, MA: Harvard University Press; London: William Heinemann, 1967).

13. This refers to the gymnasium, which was a center for learning where young men studied and exercised in the nude. For more on the history of the gymnasium and nudity in ancient Greece, please read my previous nonfiction book *Naked at Lunch: A Reluctant Nudist's Adventures in the Clothing-Optional World* (New York: Grove Press, 2015). Please. Really. I'm asking.

14. Aristophanes, *Clouds*, in *The Complete Plays*, translated by Paul Roche.

15. Philip Walsh, "A Study in Reception: The British Debates over Aristophanes' Politics and Influence," *Classical Receptions Journal* 1, no. 1 (2009): 55–72.

16. Storey, *Fragments of Old Comedy*, vol. 1.

Clouds

1. Miller, *The Colossus of Maroussi*.

2. Stephen Halliwell, trans., *Clouds, Women at the Thesmophoria, Frogs: A Verse Translation, with Introduction and Notes*, by Aristophanes (Oxford: Oxford University Press, 2015).

3. Ibid.

4. Ibid.

5. Samuel Beckett, "Worstward Ho," *Nohow On* (London: Calder, 1989).

The Arc of Comedy Bends

1. Arlene W. Saxonhouse, *Free Speech and Democracy in Ancient Athens* (Cambridge: Cambridge University Press, 2006).

2. Aristophanes, *Clouds*, in *The Complete Plays*, translated by Paul Roche.

Yanis Varoufakis Is in the House (of Parliament)

1. Paul Mason, "*Adults in the Room* by Yanis Varoufakis Review—One of the Greatest Political Memoirs Ever?," *Guardian*, May 3, 2017, https://www.theguardian.com/books/2017/may/03/yanis-varoufakis-greece-greatest-political-memoir.

Tilemachos at Sea

1. Aliki Bacopoulou-Halls, "The Theatre System of Greece," in *Theatre Worlds in Motion: Structure, Politics and Developments in the Countries of Western Europe*, edited by H. van Maanen and S. E. Wilmer (Amsterdam: Rodopi, 1998), 259–308.

2. Henri-Georges Clouzot, dir., *Le salaire de la peur* [*Wages of Fear*] (Filmsonor, 1953). Starring Yves Montand, the film tells the story of a group of desperate men trying not to blow themselves up as they drive trucks of explosives down some extremely bumpy roads.

3. Steve Rose, "Taika Waititi: 'You Don't Want to Be Directing Kids with a Swastika on Your Arm,'" *Guardian*, December 26, 2019, https://www.theguardian.com/film/2019/dec/26/taika-waititi-flight-of-the-conchords-thor-ragnarok-jojo-rabbit-nazi-dictator.

Decorative Pottery

1. For more information https://sailor-poon.bandcamp.com

2. Leslie Kurke, *Coins, Bodies, Games, and Gold: The Politics of Meaning in Archaic Greece* (Princeton, NJ: Princeton University Press, 1999).

3. Holt N. Parker, "Vaseworld: Depiction and Description of Sex at Athens," in *Ancient Sex: New Essays*, edited by Ruby Blondell and Kirk Ormand (Columbus: The Ohio State University Press, 2015), 23–142.

4. Quoted in Marguerite Johnson and Terry Ryan, *Sexuality in Greek and Roman Society and Literature* (London: Routledge, 2005).

Building Zeta

1. History of advertising department: Nicolas related a story of a prostitute who would walk through the Agora in specially designed shoes that imprinted the words "follow me" in the dirt. Her trail led to the Kerameikos.

2. Davidson, *Courtesans and Fishcakes*.

3. Parker, "Vaseworld."

Parabasis

1. James Robson, *Aristophanes: An Introduction* (London: Bloomsbury, 2009).

2. Donna Zuckerberg, *Not All Dead White Men: Classics and Misogyny in the Digital Age* (Cambridge, MA: Harvard University Press, 2018).

This Library Is on Fire

1. Matthew Battles, *Library: An Unquiet History* (New York: W. W. Norton, 2015), and *Palimpsest: A History of the Written Word* (New York: W. W. Norton, 2015).

2. William A. Johnson, *Bookrolls and Scribes in Oxyrhynchus* (Toronto: University of Toronto Press, 2013).

3. *And Tango Makes Three*, the true story of a couple of penguins in a zoo, was written by Peter Parnell and Justin Richardson, illustrated by Henry Cole (New York: Simon & Schuster, 2005).

Ta Kanaria

1. Hanink, *The Classical Debt*.

2. Vlassis Rassias, "Reclaiming the True European Identity," speech delivered at the 2014 European Congress of Ethnic Religions, Seimas of the Republic of Lithuania, Vilnius, July 9, 2014, https://ecer-org.eu/reclaiming-the-true-european-identity/.

3. Miller, *The Colossus of Maroussi*.

About the Author

Mark Haskell Smith is the author of six novels with one-word titles, including *Moist* and *Blown*, as well as the nonfiction books *Heart of Dankness* and *Naked at Lunch*. He lives in Los Angeles.

death is not yet present, and when death is present, then we do not exist."[1] Once you were dead, you were dead, which is a distinctly off-brand idea for the Church, an organization promising eternal reward in the afterlife as long as you did what it said while you were alive.

Epicurus didn't only write about pleasure; long before the invention of the electron microscope he believed that the world was made up of tiny particles, and he had profound thoughts about social justice, politics, and the corrosive nature of money. The dude was blessed with serious foresight.[2] His ideas resonated with me. After writing books about the history of nudism and the world's best cannabis, it seemed natural to explore the idea of the pursuit of pleasure as a force for social justice. I thought I would write a book on the history of pleasure, from Epicurus to the present day, and why making pleasure a priority in our lives might be the radical idea we need to halt climate change, minimize income inequality, and reimagine a life post–consumer capitalism.

I was reading historian James Davidson's remarkable book *Courtesans and Fishcakes: The Consuming Passions of Classical Athens* when I came across a throwaway line in a chapter about the drinking culture of ancient Greece. Davidson wrote: "At some point in the last quarter of the fifth century a man called Ariphrades had managed to acquire notoriety as a practitioner of cunnilingus."[3] In the context of Davidson's book, he was quoting the playwright Aristophanes, who felt that what Ariphrades did was disgusting and advised his friends not to share their wine cups with him. And that was the needle-scratch moment, when writing about the history of pleasure went caroming off the rails. My curiosity was piqued. As a fan of the practice myself, I wondered what kind of notoriety a practitioner of cunnilingus could attain. Was he really adept at it? Did he make a public nuisance of himself? And, really, why would anyone care?

that." I slid my fingers along the barrel. "If I ask God to give me another bullet, do you think he would do it?" I pointed the gun at his temple.

Father's lips jerked. His jaw twitched. A thick line of sweat coalesced along his brow.

I looked at Hannan and nudged the gun toward the door. *Hurry up.* He went to Mortimer, helped the girls lift him up the chute.

"Do you think if I have faith, enough faith, God would make a bullet appear?"

Father watched the gun with a manic intensity.

"Do you think God would do that?" The last sneakered foot disappeared. I backed toward the chute and took aim. "Do you think God would do that for me?"

SEVENTEEN

The gun didn't have bullets—of course it didn't—but sometimes you didn't need bullets. You just needed faith.

My feet moved so fast, the ground swirled in my eyes. The woods raced by, away from me.

When I reached the parking lot, Hannan, Del, Baby J, and Morty had already piled into the truck. They sat with their eyes pointed forward, as if willing it to move.

"There's no key!" Del called. "There's no key! And Morty's starting to pass out!"

"Shit." I skidded to a stop. My eyes hooked Hannan's.

The keys were with Father.

"I need to go back."

He climbed forward. "Wait. I'll go with you."

"No. Stay with Morty. See if you can hot-wire the truck. We locked him down there. He won't be able to hurt me." I think he knew that I didn't trust him, but it was more than that. I didn't trust anyone. Not even myself.

I walked up the steps to the amphitheater alone. It was the middle of the night. Somewhere far away, my fellow teenagers were probably asleep, dreaming in their beds. For once, I didn't want to be them. I was awake now. I was different, but not in the way he said I was. I was special, but not because he made me.

The path was long and my feet were heavy. The trees opened up as I crested the hill, so in a way it was like climbing toward the stars, into heaven. *You wanted us to find salvation and, in a way, I did.* I wasn't afraid anymore. I was tired and alive.

As I climbed that last step, a hollow sound escaped my lips. The trapdoor was open. The Grave yawned before me, seeming to grow larger and larger. I scanned the rows of empty stands.

"Father! I know you're out there!" My voice echoed, round and round in a circle. I climbed up onto the stage to see better. But I saw only the sky and the woods. The trees dug in their roots as if gathering their strength. Light-years away, a star winked.

The stage made me think, oddly, of my rehearsal that afternoon, and I recited the witches' lines loud and clear. " 'When shall we meet again? In thunder, lightning, or in rain? When the hurly-burly's done, when the battle's lost and won.' "

"Castley!" a voice called from the distance.

I trembled and turned to see Caspar racing up the steps. I raced down to him, because that was what the scene called for.

I put my hands on either side of his face, pressing my thumbs into his soft, clean skin.

"You're here! I thought you were—"

"Where's Father?" he said.

I twisted my head toward the sky. "I don't know. He vanished."

"The police are here. They're calling Morty an ambulance."

Officer Dell Hardy appeared, marching sideways up the steps with his gun pointed down. "Where's the shooter?"

"Gone," I said.

"You kids go back to the parking lot. This is no place for children, you understand?"

Caspar lifted me down from the stage. We passed another officer on the steps. My feet crossed without my permission. The sudden calm purred like a buzz in my ears. My head felt light. *Look at all the pretty trees.* I took Caspar's hand. "How did you know we were here?"

"Momma. Momma told us," he said.

I caught myself on his chest. "She's alive?"

He looked away. "No. But I think she wanted . . ." He stopped and hummed to delay any tears. "She said she was sorry."

"No, she didn't."

"She should have."

We passed by a tree with a white star carved into the trunk. I pulled up short, wavered on my feet. Caspar held me tight. "What is it, Castella?"

"I never carved that." I lifted my finger, indicating the narrow star. "I'm sure of it. I would remember." I dove my finger into it, pressing the point so hard my finger pulsed.

"Someone else must've carved it," he said.

"But who? Who did it?"

He held me against him, so tight our hearts doubled. "Does it matter?"

"No." I sighed. "I guess it doesn't."

SPRING

We were on the roof again, helping clear Ms. Sturbridge's rain gutters. Ms. Sturbridge was making lemonade, even though it was barely spring and we were still in coats and jackets.

Mortimer was down below arguing with Uncle Michael about something he'd seen on TV. Hannan and Delvive were at church with Emily Higgins. Jerusalem was standing just below us with her easel, painting the house as we balanced on top of it.

If someone had told me six months ago that we would all be there together like that, I never would have believed it. I never could have seen it. But that's what life is like; it blinds you. It makes you think you'll never escape. But you will. You will if you keep fighting, even if sometimes you don't know what you're fighting for.

"The trees look so pretty, don't they?" Amity said, coming up behind me. "With all their new leaves?"

I shivered. I hadn't been thinking about the trees. I had been thinking about someone I knew who had disappeared. Disappeared, never to be found, dead or alive. I caught Caspar's eye and I knew he was thinking the same thing.

"Yes," I agreed. "They look pretty." I got back to work.

I used to think you were meant to learn something from everything, that life was one great big lesson, but I don't think that's true anymore.

I guard my mind and my heart, because you have to be careful what you learn; you have to be careful who you let in. Some people might look pretty or talk prettily, but it's the things they do that tell you if they're worthy of your time. It's the things they do that tell you if they deserve your faith.

ACKNOWLEDGMENTS

Lo + behold, god willing, you will get there to the other side of life and find happiness that every man craves, love, life + freedom.
—Alan Wass

I have to wonder what the point is in writing a thank-you to someone who will never read it, but wherever you are, in time or space or somewhere just outside it, this book wouldn't exist without you. I wouldn't exist without you, because I would be someone else, and thanks to you, I'm a better version of myself. You believed in me, you supported me, you inspired me, you drove me crazy, but most of all you loved me, all of me, for who I was and who I wanted to be, instead of what you wanted from me. This book, and everything I am, is for you, always.

Thank you to Hortensia Perez, who helped me send my first book to a random Hollywood address we found online. I told you something would happen. Wish you were here to see it.

Thank you to my editor, Emily Meehan, and her assistant, Hannah Allaman; my copy editor, Kate Hurley; my cover artist, Maria E. Elias; and the team at Hyperion.

Thank you to my agents, Madeleine Milburn and Cara Simpson.

Thank you to my parents, Kit and Jim,

My siblings, Tim, Noah, Seth, Christina, Emma, Beverly, Colton, and Thomas,

My Brazier-in-laws, Carrie, Kiersten, Shayne, Josh, Brad, Nick, and Cassie,

My Brazier nephews and nieces, Elena, Lydia, Rocky, Boston, Jonah, Rachel, Abram, Nigel, Chase, Georgiana, Sienna, Charlie, Ezra, Eli, Peter, Henri Alan, and Grant,

And the Wass family, Chris, Angela, Mandy, Caroline, Alison, Vanessa, Fab, Josh, Lillie, Harry, and Leo,

For all their love and support.

A special thanks to EVERYONE I've connected with on Twitter. This book came together thanks to your support, advice, and critiques, sometimes in a DM, sometimes in a tweet. Thank you for teaching me that wherever I am, whatever I'm going through, there is always someone out there to talk to, to rant to, to share in this wonderful, torturous experience we call writing (and sometimes, by its lesser name, "life").

To the readers, I can't wait to hear from you. You're the reason I started writing to begin with (and the reason I wrote a shit-ton of fan fiction). All this publishing business is just a way to get this story to YOU.

I would also like to thank the future, for being just beyond our reach, and for tantalizing us with the possibilities of what we can one day be.